WE ARE TWINS BUT WHO AM I ?

Betty Jean Case

Portland, Oregon
Tibbutt Publishing Company
1991

Cataloging in Publication Data
Case, Betty Jean.
    We are twins, but who am I/ Betty Jean Case. — Portland,
OR: Tibbutt Pub. Co., 1991

    v, 203 p. : ill. ; 23cm.

Includes bibliographical references (p. 194-195) and index.

    ISBN 0-9629948-0-4

1. Twins—psychology. 2. Identity (psychology) 3. Self-respect.
I. Title.

BF723.T9   155.4'44 dc 20
                                                    00-

Library of Congress Card Number 91-65981

This book may not be reproduced in whole or in part, by mimeograph or any other means,
without permission. For information address:
Tibbutt Publishing Company, Inc.,
0438 S. W. Palatine Hill Road
Portland, Oregon 97219

For my twin grandsons, Andy and Tony, who inspired me to write this book, and for all twins everywhere.

Acknowledgments

Over the past nine years I have been immersed with thoughts and experiences shared by identical and fraternal twins. Into my life have come a host of people I would never have known had I not delved into the world of twins. Many of them I have come to know personally. The majority I know only on paper.

It is impossible to thank all of them personally for their thoughts and contributions to this book, but I want everyone who has helped with information to know I am grateful.

To all of you who showed an interest in my research, or who played any part in the book's creation, I want to say thank you for your support and your caring. You know who you are.

I have been touched by the cooperation I've had from the National Organization of Mothers of Twins Clubs. Inc., the International Twins Association participants, and other twin organizations. They have taught me what the bond of twin fellowship is all about.

My appreciation also to Twins Magazine for a wealth of information which has enlarged my knowledge of twins.

I am grateful to my family and friends for their

understanding when I was unable to be more a part of their lives. Also to Alexandra Jean, Jocelyn Ann and Johnna Lynn who didn't really understand why "Grammy" couldn't come and play more.

My husband Laurel has been my constant and patient sounding board and always a loving supporter. Without him I never would have made it.

Thorn Bacon is the professional writer who showed up at the right time. Without his expert guidance on how to focus the book and use my material to best advantage, I fear the book would never have been written. Also, I wish to thank Ursula Bacon and Dari Smith for their editorial assistance.

The author, her sister, mother and brothers. Top left Torrence Ness (Tod) and Theodore Van (Ted). Betty Jean and her sister Fay Louise are in the basket at the bottom. Their mother was Fay Van Ness Tibbutt.

Introduction

I was expected to be a single birth but my sister made me a twin.

If I had not become the grandmother to twin boys I doubt that I would ever have given more than a passive thought to my own twinship and how being a twin has made me a different person than I would have been if I'd been born a single child.

The library was my first stop in search of answers to my question. I was interested in the psychological aspects of twinship; how twins felt about being twins and how they felt that being a twin had affected their lives. When I realized that the answers were not there I decided to go to the twins themselves. I did not know if they would be willing to tell me, a total stranger, their very intimate thoughts about such a personal subject.

I asked twins the very questions for which I wanted answers myself. To my surprise I found that other twins were also anxious to learn more about twins and about their relationship with their twin. Where did I find the twins? Everywhere. My antenna was out day and night. I found them as clerks in all kinds of stores, airports, trains, motels, churches, through friends, other twins, twin organizations and at parties. Wherever there is a large group of people there are twins, though you may not always be aware of it.

After I began to hear from other twins, I realized that I was not alone in my quest for answers. It was then I felt I had a contribution to make to twins and that I owed it to them to let them know what I had learned from their counterparts.

This book then, is by a twin, about twins, and for twins---but not JUST for twins. It is also for parents and families of twins, for friends and teachers and anyone else who encounters twins or who shares the common fascination with this closest of all human relationships.

Through the sharing of each others' reflections, memories and opinions, you, my twin readers may learn---as I did---that "we are indeed not alone." You may discover ways to nurture each other's self-esteem through acting as advocates and supporters for each other.

Parents, families, and friends may see the effects, both positive and negative, of certain ways of relating to twins. Perhaps this will help you to make better decisions about how to encourage their individual growth and to enrich your relationship with them.

Teachers and other school personnel may learn to counter the common expectation that twins are to be treated as "halves of a whole." You may discover help in evaluating each set of twins separately, to decide how they may be most effectively and humanely dealt with both in and out of the classroom.

The non-twin reader may identify with personal issues which are not unique to twinship, but which are intensified by it.

You may find yourself empathizing with the twins you meet here, feeling more prepared to deal sensitively not only with twins, but with each new individual you encounter. If such increased empathy brings about more nurturing of self-esteem for you and for those you meet, then the question in my title *We Are Twins, But Who Am I ?* will have an answer.

TABLE OF CONTENTS

CHAPTER I

I Was Born A Twin

I was born a twin. In fact, all the children in my family arrived in pairs---twin boys first, followed four years later by my sister and myself. For most of my life, I gave little thought to how this accident of birth affected my development, my image of myself, and my self-esteem.

I always took my twinship for granted, as I took for granted that I was born female. Why would I need to examine my twinship---didn't I already know all about it, having been born a twin? Why analyze something that was such a "given" in my life?

It took the birth of twin grandsons and my reactions to how other people treated them to start me wondering if my frequent feelings of inferiority and self-doubt had been inspired by similar treatment when I was a child.

One incident in particular became the catalyst for a process that led to six years of often-painful self-analysis, extensive

1

research, and struggle with inner doubts about my ability to carry out the project I had undertaken.

It was necessary for me to explore the effect of having felt, for most of my life, like one-half (or less) of a pair, before I could finally experience myself as a whole and worthy individual. This book is the result of that exploration.

Through it, I hope to assist other twins (and those who share their lives) with their own process of becoming whole, separate and complete individuals who happen to share one of the most unique and potentially-rewarding bonds two human beings can have.

The pivotal incident began innocently enough with an eagerly-anticipated visit from my son, his wife, and their eight-month-old twin boys. Their stay coincided with a rare visit from my own twin sister, with whom I had felt very close as a child, but with whom I had often felt a puzzling and painful sense of distance as an adult.

My own sons had been born four-and-a-half-years apart, so this was my first exposure to two small beings of the same age, who at one time required basically the same care, yet who even now possessed remarkably different wants and needs.

Just a few days before their arrival at my home, one twin had discovered that getting up on all fours made for much greater mobility than creeping on his stomach. One day, during their visit, he emerged from the nursery, going full speed down the hallway, leaving his twin brother far behind. Who said it, I don't know, but I heard: "Wow, he sure has mastered the art of crawling. Look at him go! He's really leaving his brother behind."

"Comparison!" The word leapt into my mind, if not from my mouth. Like the other observers, I found myself doing it automatically, unthinkingly. At the same time, I found myself inwardly cringing for the one following, already labeled with the "slower" image those words implied---an image that, blessedly, he was still too young to comprehend. Or was he?

At that moment, in my mind, the clock raced back to the little brown house where my twin and I were born more than 60 years ago. In my strong reaction to the comparing of my grandchildren was I really seeing my twin sister making progress toward the open door which represented opportunity and adult approval, while I still lay there crying because I wanted to move too, but hadn't yet developed the skill to do just what she was doing?

Concern for the possible negative effect of comparisons on my grandsons mingled in my mind with emerging questions about myself: Had my twin and I once been the focus of such comparison, and at what age did I become aware of them? Was I, even in my 60's still being compared, or comparing myself, with my twin? Was that at the root of my deeply-ingrained feeling of being less attractive, less smart, less capable, less friendly, less everything, than my twin? And what was the effect of such comparisons on my sister? Was there some unacknowledged competition between us that blocked the bond of mutual affection I so wanted us to share?

Since my twin and I are fraternal, we look less alike than many siblings of different ages. As children, we often heard the comment: "You two don't look like twins!" But once our twinship was known, comparisons frequently followed. Usually they were well-meant, but often the effect was painful. The innocent question: "What grade are you in?" was a continuing source of anguish for me. It was rarely explained that I was a grade behind my sister because of absences due to a series of illnesses in fourth grade; I simply felt the shame of being seen as the "slower" twin.

How would my two little grandsons respond to the same

questions that had so often been asked of my sister and I: "Are you two twins?" "What grade are you in?" "Who is taller?" "Which one is better at math?"

I thought about comparisons. Just what is it that can make them so damaging to the human psyche? After all, the ability to perceive differences is a basic skill, necessary for successful learning and functioning in the world. Why should it matter if one twin is taller, or can run faster, or excels in a certain subject at school? If one is outgoing, the other reserved, is that strange?

I came to realize that if *value judgments* were not implied in comparisons, then surely they could do no harm. But that's a big "if". In noting the differences between people, how many of us are able to avoid giving subtle signals, a nod of approval, a slight change of voice, that one quality is more or less desirable than another? The need to judge, to rank, to prioritize is deeply ingrained in our culture and in our selves. And how many of us are so inwardly secure in our sense of personal worth that our self-images are unaffected by the evaluations, spoken or unspoken, of others?

I began to ponder the question of self-esteem, and how it might be affected by twinship. Are there experiences unique to twins that may impede the growth of their self-esteem as individuals? Are the effects of comparisons, expectations, jealousy, or favoritism more pronounced on twin's self-esteem than on other siblings?

I found myself asking: "Did my past experiences as a twin cause the shaky self-esteem that is still affecting how I function, how I deal with the issues of life?

Self-esteem is such an important aspect of being; its lack can hold a person captive who has much to offer. The need to feel good about oneself is vital, to be able to function and to be productive in the world. How much more might I have accomplished in my life, if I'd only believed myself more capable? Would my twin grandsons's self-esteem be

4

threatened just because another person happened to share their day of birth?

This introspection led to much soul-searching, as the desire grew in me to work through my own self-esteem problems arising from twinship, and to understand the pain I was still experiencing in my relationship with my twin.

What, I wondered, are the issues that contribute to healthy self-esteem, or to its absence, in a child? Are twins treated differently than other children because of their twinship? What is the effect on family relationships when there are two children the same age? Is having a "built-in playmate" a help or a hindrance to individual growth? If one twin is favored, how are both affected? Are certain issues of greater importance for identical twins than for fraternals, and vice versa? Do the issues change as twins grow older and their life paths diverge through career, marriage, and parenthood? If twins are able to carry the closeness of childhood into adulthood and old age, is it a matter of luck, proper guidance, or something else?

These thoughts led to a desire to find out what other twins had experienced. My research turned up virtually no published material on adult twins' feelings about their twinship. So I devised a questionnaire, asking about issues that were deeply relevant to me, personally. I mailed it to more than 800 twins---identical and fraternal, male and female, in the U.S. and in other countries.

The responses were overwhelming in their honesty and their length. I was deeply touched by the sharing of these strangers' personal experiences and their feelings about them. I discovered I was not alone in feeling "second best", often both twins felt that sense of inadequacy!

As the responses poured in, often with added pages of handwritten comments and enouragement, the feeling grew in me that I had something important to share. I came to believe there was a great need among twins for a book about their personal experiences of twinship.

To fill that need became my challenge---a vehicle for my personal growth which has forced me to confront all my own fears and feelings of inadequacy from the past, and to overcome them.

My research has convinced me more than ever of the importance of nurturing self-esteem in all individuals. It has also shown that certain aspects of twinship---mostly the ways in which other people respond to twins---can often have negative effects on the twins' development of self-esteem as separate, whole individuals. While the vast majority of twins I've encountered value their unique bond with their partner-in-birth, most agree that the bond creates special problems as well.

Thus, my overall goal for this book is to suggest and illustrate ways to help build and nurture twins' self-esteem through recognition of each twin as a unique individual. Through sharing my experiences and those of the hundreds of twins who answered my questions, I hope to achieve the following objectives:

*To increase the general awareness of how twinship is different from other sibling relationships and of how twinship affects every area of personality and experience.

*To encourage dialogue and communication between twins about their feelings, thoughts, and experiences, and thus ultimately to help them have the richest relationship possible.

*To persuade parents and others of the importance of treating each twin as an individual, separate and unique.

I hope that the reader will draw the same overall conclusion I have drawn from my experiences and from my research: *Happy Are Those Twins Who Are Free To Be Themselves.* I believe the same could be said for all human beings. This book is an attempt to help record, interpret and promulgate the process by which twins learn to free themselves.

It may prove to be inspirational to all growing individuals who wish to be themselves.

In the following chapter, we will look at what makes twins unique and how research is proving that the awesome similarities between some twins is leading to new understanding of the remarkable potential for the expansion of human growth.

CHAPTER II

Living As A Twin

We are ever intrigued by twins. Two peas in the same pod fascinate us. They look alike, therefore they are different from us. By learning about this difference, about the emotions and behavior of two people who may be closer in their feelings than any other humans can be, we can, perhaps, better understand our own humanity and find ways to improve it.

This natural curiosity became the subject of an outstanding University of Minnesota study of twins that has revolutionized the way we view heredity. We have learned that it plays the key role as the master conductor of the symphony of life. It sets the stage for how we think and act.

If the study of identical twins reared apart can lead us to some of the secrets of human behavior, then being a twin takes on greater importance today because in the two halves of a whole there exists the marvelous opportunity of valid comparison for such traits as musical ability, temperament, leadership and even the inclination to become teary-eyed over a sad movie.

The Minnesota study of Twins Reared Apart was begun in 1979 by Doctor Thomas J. Bouchard, Jr., University of Minnesota psychologist who started with Jim Lewis and Jim Springer, Ohio twins who were raised in different homes. The men volunteered to undergo exhaustive testing that involved thousands of questions. What emerged about the two was fascinating:

* Both men had identical blood pressures, pulse rates, sleep patterns, and psychological inventory profiles.

* Each married women named Linda, divorced them and took second wives named Betty.

* Tension/migraine headaches, the same brand of cigarettes, a preference for Chevrolets, vacations on the same Florida beach, wood working as a past time and nail biting as a nervous habit, are some of the remarkable shared experiences of Jim Lewis and Jim Springer.

* Both men built a white bench around the tree in his yard, and both reported a fascination with math in school and a dislike for spelling. So far, more than 106 pairs of reared-apart twins have been tested in the Minnesota study, 65 percent of them identical. Every one of the pairs has demonstrated parallel behaviors and personality traits.

One of the participants in my 1982 twins survey of attitudes, a man named Eric of Portland, Oregon, expressed the closeness identical twins feel, a sharing that people who are not twins often envy:

"To be a twin is to share a special form of consciousness. Sharing the same genetic material, DNA, childhood, similar thoughts, is an experience most people don't understand. Even a marriage may not be as close as being a twin."

In overwhelming numbers, whether they have been reared apart or together, twins are glad to be twins. Tim Carpenter and Bill Henry are Rhode Island identical twins who did not discover one another until friends of each accidentically brought them together. Tim was often confused when he was addressed as "Bill", not realizing that the person speaking to him was mistaking him for his unknown twin brother. A football game in Cranston, Rhode Island was the occasion when Bill and Tim found one another. The meeting was dramatic and changed the lives of both men. They discovered later uncanny similarities in their lives.

The boys learned they had been adopted by different families after birth and for sixteen years their lives were like other kids, each living in an adoptive family with a brother for one and a sister for the other.

"Our lives were probably easier in many ways because we lived apart. If we had been raised in one home, like other twins, there would have been a constant hassle to be different from the other twin," Tim said.

Researchers have discovered that twins like Bill and Tim who have grown to maturity without the pervasive influence of an identical twin to modify behavior are actually more similar to one another than those who have been raised together.

As Alice Vollmer, a writer whose subject often is twins, wrote, "Twins raised separately have no chance to interact or be compared to one another. Twins growing up together often work to create identities distinct from one another. To cut down on comparisons, they may choose different activities, friends or clothing."

Fascination with the dualism in twins raised independent of one another as demonstrated by their patterns of thinking, behavior,

10

dressing, marriage customs, brand of cigarettes and marked preferences for such innocuous items as hair brushes, toothpaste and neckties, impelled Dr. Bouchard to observe from his twins study that environment provides the "precipitating factors" in development of human life. Predisposing factors are those, says Bouchard, that we inherit from the gene combinations passed on to us by our parents.

Since science postulates theories based on repetitive observation of data, Bouchard and his associates were both shocked and delighted with the Minnesota studies of reared-apart twins. Among them were female twins, each of whom wore three rings on one hand and four on the other. One sister had named her son Andrew Richard, while the other named her son Richard Andrew.

Keith and Dale Edwards, Medford, Oregon twins who answered survey questions I sent to them, reported that they used to communicate mentally while separated from one another. Occasionally they confused co-workers by demonstrating parallel thoughts while completely out of sight of one another.

Here then seems to be evidence that heredity plays a dominant role in the selection of traits which a person uses to manage his life. Environment, on the other hand, is the bow drawn across the strings of human endowment.

"I tell parents," says Bouchard, "to look at their children as guests. You should recognize that your kids are born with certain tendencies. It's your job to identify and bolster the good ones and teach them how to control the bad ones."

He cautions parents to remember that each one of us represents an entirely new genetic configuration and that biological determinism in the archaic and rigid sense of being doomed by heredity is as outmoded as the Model-T.

Probably the most important aspect of the Minnesota studies is the refreshing light they have cast on the uniqueness of twins. They have created a broad new surge of interest in twins and the dawning realization that observation of identical twins especially can help us to understand ourselves better.

This spotlight comes at a time when multiple births have been steadily rising. During the period 1982-1986 total live births increased by 3.8 %, while multiple births rose 14.3 percent. Cause of the twin boom is attributed to the increased number of mothers in their thirties. Women 35 to 39 are three to five times as likely as younger women to release more than one egg when they ovulate. Multiple ovulation in older women is probably nature's way of insuring the survival of at least one baby.

Another reason for the overall increase in twins is simply that more twin babies are surviving being born. Twins, often premature, are being saved today by doctors who have learned how. Experts say more twins are in our future. As long as women postpone pregnancy this trend will continue.

The process which leads to twins is one that continues to fascinate, and while medical science can now predict fairly reliably the conception of twins, the news is always greeted with amazement and consternation.

Fraternal twins are conceived when the mother releases two eggs from her ovaries and each one is fertilized by a different sperm. Of the 40,000 sets of twins born each year in the United States two thirds of them are fraternal twins, dizygotic (two eggs). Fraternal twins each have their own individual set of genes and they resemble one another as much or as little as any sisters and brothers do. Of all fraternal twins, half are of the same sex and half are of the opposite sex.

The conception of fraternal twins is more likely if certain factors are present. Age of the mother is one factor---35 to 40 years old--- and mothers who have given birth several times are even more likely to produce fraternal twins. This is caused by an increase in the hormone that stimulates the release of the eggs from the ovaries.

If a woman has already given birth to fraternal twins, her chances of having another set quadruple. The incidence of fraternal twins is also related to race; it is highest among blacks and lowest among orientals. This is probably due to different levels of hormones among women of distinct races. Another factor that increases the chances of bearing twins is heredity. The propensity to release more than one egg per cycle is believed to be inherited from the mother's side of the family. Since the 1950s when the fertility drugs, Clomid and Perganol were introduced that stimulate the release of eggs from the ovaries more twins have been born and more multiple births have occurred. Babies born as a result of these hormones are always fraternal twins.

The conception of identical twins is more mysterious. Monozygotic (one egg) twins happen when a single egg is released and fertilized, then doubles in chromosomes and for unknown reasons splits into equal halves. Each half of the egg carries the same genes and chromosomes as the other half. Identical twins are always of the same sex and their facial features, eye and hair color and blood groups are the same. Although their handprints and footprints are very much alike, the fingerprints of each identical twin are always unique.

Science has not yet discovered what causes an egg to split. While this remains unsolved the incidence of identical twins seems to be the same around the world. Another type of twin may be a combination of fraternal and identical. Researchers theorize that some twins result from the fertilization of a single egg by two different sperm. In this case, half of the twins' genes would be

The Process By Which The Zygosity Of Identical And Fraternal Twins Is Determined.

NONIDENTICAL TWINS

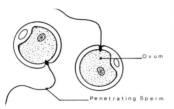

Nonidentical twins come from two separate ova that have been fertilized by two separate spermatozoa.

IDENTICAL TWINS

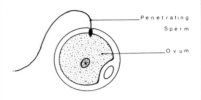

Identical twins come from a single fertilized ovum. When the ovum splits the two cells formed develop independently.

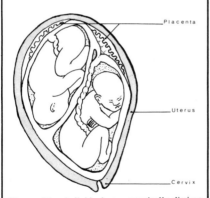

The resulting individuals are genetically distinct and have separate placentas. They are dizygotic or binovular twins.

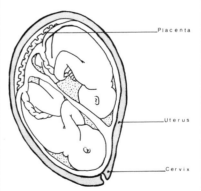

The result is a pair of genetically identical twins sharing the same placenta. They are called monovular or monozygotic.

identical---deriving from the egg, and half would be different---
deriving from two different sperms.

The famous Chicago dispute of 1938 between two men
both of whom claimed to be the father of a set of boy/girl twins
demonstrated another kind of multiple birth. Blood tests showed
that either--- or both---might be the father, calling into account the
theory of superfecundation, a weighty description of an unusual
process in which two eggs released in the same cycle are fertilized
by two sperm released in two separate sexual acts.

The Chicago fathers, unable to agree to a judicial suggestion
that the twins be divided between them, had to submit to the wisdom
of the court in settlement of their claims of paternity.

Multiple births is the abiding interest of "Miss Helen" Kirk
of Galveston, Texas, who has become known as the statistician of
mothers who produce two or more babies. According to Kirk, her
records reveal a Texas woman who delivered an astonishing number
and arrangement of multiples: One set of quintuplets, one set of
quadruplets, five sets of twins, three sets of triplets, and nine single
children. In all 37 babies!

Perhaps the most fascinating aspect of multiple births is the
mystery of the vanishing twin. Some men and women report having
experienced a distinct feeling of loss or separation from a part of
themselves which they can't explain. The feeling often is equivalent
in intensity on an emotional level to the accident victim who has lost
a leg and feels its invisible presence even though it no longer exists.
This emotional separation has been attributed by some physicians to
the phenomenon known as the "vanishing twin process". This refers
to the fact that many of us actually may have started life in the
womb with a twin who for some reason did not survive and was
reabsorbed into the tissues of the mother's body.

Baffling as this may appear to be, as far back as 1945 there were references in the medical literature to the vanishing twin but the idea could not be developed until the perfection of ultrasound. Now, medical investigators have discovered that conception of twins happens more often than previously thought. There is routine evidence available to substantiate that in many cases a second twin of an original pair died in utero and was absorbed by the tissues of the womb in a manner similar to a sponge sucking up water without changing its form.

Twins are popular subjects of research for a variety of reasons. Primarily, we are interested in them because they represent a "couple effect" that, intriguingly, offers a convenient standard of measurement of the closest kind of personal communication between two humans.

Because they are so similar, twins develop secret languages, systems of signalling to one another, reduced sociability and often delayed mental development. While identical twins are encouraged to grow individually, some of them are so dependent upon one another that the challenge of developing the self becomes a problem.

"I never made a bed alone, washed dishes alone or cleaned a room alone until I married, or shopped alone until I was married. I suppose you would call that dependency and I transferred that to my husband." wrote an identical woman who was part of my twin study. Adding to her comments, she said: "I think I depended on my twin sister too much growing up and I still depend upon her now, mostly for my social life. I feel that I can't seem to think for myself, I discuss everything with my sister. Decision-making is hard for me, but I don't know if that has anything to do with being a twin."

While fraternal twins do not usually develop the closeness and psychological interdependence that identical twins do, intense bonds do develop and they illustrate the special rapprochement that

15

exists between twins. This was demonstrated in the statement made by Princess Ashraf Pahlavi in her memoir, *Faces in A Mirror.* Writing of the relationship with her brother Mohamed Reza, the Shah Of Iran, she said, "This twinship and this relationship with my brother...would nurture and sustain me throughout my childhood (and) would constitute the strongest sense of family that I would ever know. No matter how I would reach out in the years to come--- sometimes even desperately---to find an identity and purpose of my own, I would remain inextricably tied to my twin brother."

The eloquence with which Princess Ashraf described her longing to be a person of her own while tied by affection and love for her brother brings to a point the dilemma of twins, torn by loyalty and tugged by the desire for independence. In choosing the title of this book, I, who am a fraternal twin, thought there could be no more appropriate expression of the struggle of twinship than the refrain, We Are Twins, But Who Am I ?

I have spoken with hundreds of twins and most of them in one way or another, have expressed a need for a true sense of their individual selves. Often, it is difficult and emotionally crippling for twins to pull away from one another. And, marriage, the ultimate symbol of release from twinship, may be the most traumatic division of the "couple" whose struggle to modify their relationship often leaves scars and feelings of rejection. Indicative of the ambivalence with which many twins view marriage are the statistics which show that 25% of identical male twins remain unmarried; 46% of fraternal male, female twins remain celibate and 47% of identical female twins remain unmarried. In the population at large 16% of all males and 26% of all females remain unmarried. The comparison of statistics shows the resistance of twins to the modification of the "couple" relationship they have nurtured since birth.

16

An identical twin woman who participated in my survey of twins acknowledged the difficulty she had adjusting to marriage.

"Marriage is made more difficult by a tug of loyalties," she said. "Part of me will, even now, feel that I must come to the aid of my sister, even when it isn't to the advantage of my husband and children. Since I was used to thinking in terms of 'we' for everything it was probably easier to move into a marriage relationship.

Another twin, an identical woman, observed, "I was always used to sharing everything, time, energy, ideas, things. I just continued to do so. However, many years later I realized that I did not develop myself individually which is related to being a twin. It is hard for me to know what 'I' liked, what 'I' wanted. How 'I' felt. Those 'I's' were not a part of my thinking. It has only been in the later years of my life that I became just 'ME'. This has, of course, had a negative impact on my own development and therefore the marriage relationship."

While twins develop a relationship that is more intellectually parallel than other humans, the matter of individual identity is important because of the very human desire for recognition.

This was put in perspective by one of a pair of twins who wrote that she and her sister have often wondered which of them was born first and which name was proper for each child. Anita said their mother told them that she was cautioned not to remove their baby bracelets while bathing them when they were infants. Without thinking she did remove the bracelets and failed to remind herself to replace them on the babies' wrists in proper sequence after she dried them. Years later the question arose as to which twin was Anita and which was Vanita. The twins' mother remembered that Anita was more darkly complected when she was born.

Yet, it was the grownup twin named Vanita who had the darker complexion.

It may not seem important that the names of twins are accidentally exchanged when they are infants, but we are creatures of detail and measurement. Small things give us comfort and security. The knowledge of who was born first or last provides us with a sense of place in the family. Of course, it is even more important for twins and their parents to determine whether the offspring are identical or fraternal. Hinging on this difference may be medical decisions that could mean life or death.

Elinor Davis, parent, former nurse and writer, tells of a three-year- old girl, Jenny, who was burned and required skin grafts on her arm and leg. The worried parents gave physicians permission for blood tests to determine if Jenny's sister, Cara, was an identical or fraternal twin. Up to the time Jenny was burned, they had never been certain of the zygosity of the girls.

Happily, Jenny and Cara proved to be identical twins. This meant that a skin transplant could be done without any danger of rejection. Successful transplants are only possible between identical twins.

Knowing the twins' zygosity is useful because it helps families to understand the twins and the twins to understand each other. Research on twin development tells us that generalizations about identicals do not necessarily apply to fraternals, and vice versa. Parents can expect identicals to be very similar in interest, abilities, appearance, temperament and health. In studies of puzzle solving,identicals tend to be less competitive and more cooperative with each other than fraternals. They may have a harder time separating and establishing individual identities as adults, partly because others see them as a unit. Fraternal twins also share a special and close relationship, but because they are less alike,

18

generally have less difficulty differentiating from each other.

For these reasons and others, it is always important to know as much about your children as possible. The distinction between fraternal and identical twins is crucial because in the final analysis it will aid parents in determining their own expectations of their twins. It is useful to remember that identical, or monozygotic, twins result when one fertilized egg splits to form two or more babies with exactly the same genetic inheritance. Any differences between them are assumed to be due to environment, including prenatal experiences. Fraternal or dizygotic twins develop from two separate eggs and are as similar or dissimilar as any brothers or sisters. Boy-girl twins are always fraternal.

Blood tests have largely replaced placental examination to determine genetic identity. This is important information since two thirds of all twins are of the same sex. The belief was common for a long time that twins born from one placenta were one-egg twins, while those born from two placentas were two-egg twins. Medical science now knows that identicals may develop separate placentas and that the placentas of fraternal twins may even fuse together. Placental formations can provide strong clues about zygosity. It is a good idea to consult your doctor about the procedures for developing this information.

Parents can also learn a great deal about their twins by comparing their physical features and personalities. Eyes are the best indicators of zygosity. Identical twins have the same eye color and patterns of lines and dots in the iris. Other similar features in monozygotic twins are the color, texture and distribution of hair, skin texture and pigmentation, teeth, shape of ears, size of hands and feet, foot and handprints and blood groups. If there are major differences in more than one of these, it is likely that the twins are fraternal.

19

The object of discovery about twins is to free them from attitudes that place them in a category of the strange. Each one of us comes into the world with a unique heredity. Some twins may share an identical genetic blueprint that makes it possible for us to observe dualism as it holds up a reflecting mirror. By applying what we discover about ourselves from twins, we may learn to create a better humanity in a world that grows smaller every day.

The National Organization of Mothers of Twins Clubs, Inc. provided an exceptional service for twins when it printed a valuable glossasry of frequently used terms or explanations relating to twins. It was compiled by Charlotte Hradek. The data to provide this information was gathered by the organization from a variety of sources. The glossary is printed here with permission of NOMOTC. It answers questions twins may have about themselves and is useful as a dependable resource. The title Glossary of Multiple Birth Terms is my own.

*****
Glossary of Multiple Birth Terms

CONCEPTION: The union of the male sperm and the ovum of the female; fertilization.

ZYGOTE: The cell resulting from union of a male and a female gamete, until it divides; the fertilized ovum.

ZYGOSITY; Number of eggs fertilized in a given pregnancy; in the case of twin, whether developing from one zygote (monozygosity) or two (dizygosity).

MONOZYGOTIC (MZ): Pertaining to or derived from one fertilized ovum (zygote), as identical twins.

DIZYGOTIC(DZ): Pertaining to or derived from two separate zygotes, as fraternal twins.

GESTATION: From the time of fertilization of the ovum until birth.

MULTIPLE GESTATION: To bear or carry more than one fetus from the time of fertilization until birth: carrying more than one fetus during a single pregnancy.

MULTIPLE BIRTH: The birth of two or more offspring produced in the same gestation period.

PRENATAL: Occurring shortly before and shortly after birth, with reference to the fetus: defined as beginning with completion of the 20th to 28th week of gestation and ending 7 to 28 days after birth.

PREPARTAL: Occurring before, or just previous to, labor.

INTRAPARTUM: Occurring during childbirth or delivery.

POSTNATAL: Occurring after childbirth, or after delivery, with reference to the newborn.

POSTPARTUM: Occurring after childbirth, or after delivery, with reference to the mother.

TWINS: Two babies born at one birth, occurring one in 90 births.

TRIPLETS: Three babies born at one birth, occurring once in approximately 9,300 births.

QUADRUPLETS: Four babies born at one birth, occurring once in every
190,000 births.

QUINTUPLETS: Five babies born at one birth, occurring once in every 55,000,000 births.

SUPERTWINS: Term used to refer to more than twins; for example, triplets, quadruplets, quintuplets.

COTWIN: A twin: term used in twin studies to identify pairs of twins, one of a twin pair.

SIBLING: One of two or more children of same parents; a brother or sister.

SINGLETON: One only, as distinguished from more than one; an individual, not a twin, triplet or quadruplet.

IDENTICAL TWINS, MONOZYGOTIC (MZ): Result when a single fertilized egg splits usually 1 to 14 days after conception. These twins are genetically alike. Identical twinning is a biological phenomenon and the incidence remains fairly constant throughout the world. Identical twins have the same chromosomes and usually have remarkable physical similarities but are not entirely identical. Each twin is an individual and has unique traits of his own. Identical twins are the same sex, the same blood type and have the same hair and eye color, same nose, ear and lip shapes.

FRATERNAL, DIZYGOTIC (DZ): Result from two fertilized eggs and are not necessarily any more alike than any two singletons born to the same parents. They may or may not be of the same sex. The tendency to bear fraternal twins may be inherited from either side of the family. The incidence of fraternal twinning is affected by heredity, race, maternal age and number of children previously borne.

OPPOSITE-SEX (BOY/GIRL) TWINS: Comprise one-third of the twin population, approximately one in 240 births. Always fraternal twins. Boy, girl twins develop as differently as males and females differ biologically from the time of conception. Males tend to be heavier and longer than females both before and after birth. Growth is faster in males than females until about 7 months of age, at which time females begin to grow faster until about the age of 4 years.

Girls are generally shorter and lighter than boys of the same age until they are about 18 years old. Males excel in muscle development, have a higher basal metabolism, larger heart and lungs. A newborn female displays a level of physical maturity that is typical of a four to six- week-old male. Development of bones and teeth occurs earlier in females than males. Females, on the average, tend to sit, crawl and walk at an earlier age than males. Males show earlier visual skills while females show greater auditory skills. Female infants appear more sensitive than male infants to crying of other babies in a nursery situation. Females social behavior shows greater cooperation, helping behaviors. Males engage more frequently in physical activities such as running. Four year old boys tend to organize themselves into larger social groups than girls. Boys are louder, more frenzied and more disorganized. Girls, however, boy/girl twin pairs are more similar, on the average, then non-twin pairs on most mathematical and language tests. Studies have shown that boy/girl twins have fewer problems with either their twins or the school authorities in regard to placement in the same or separate classrooms at school.

MIRROR-IMAGE TWINS; Reversed asymmetry: thought to occur when the embryo suddenly splits, well past the point that the embryo has begun to differentiate right and left sides. This usually results in opposite swirls of the hair, handedness, etc. In extreme cases, the internal organs are reversed in one of the twins. One in four identical twins are mirror-image. Siamese twins show a high degree of mirror-imaging.

SIAMESE TWINS: Conjoined twins: formed by a late separation of identical (MZ) twin conceptions; extremely rare; occur 1 in 50,000 to 1 in 100,000 births; three times more likely to be girls than boys. Siamese twins joined at the head is the rarest form; occurring about 1 in 2.5 million births. Joined at the chest is most common form and is found in 70% of Siamese twins.

FERTILITY: The capacity to conceive or induce conception.

IN-VITRO FERTILIZATION: Technique where fertilization takes place within a glass, dish or tube, in an artificial environment, and then resulting embyos placed in the woman's uterus. Artificially induced twins are always fraternal.

FERTILITY DRUGS: Drugs taken to stimulate ovulation. Thirty-one percent of mothers responding to NOMOTC's "Fertility Drug Study" conducted in 1986 felt that they had conceived with the help of fertility drugs. The fertility drug used most frequently was Clomid although others were used including Follutein, Pergonol, Depo-Provera and Provera. Other drugs are also available. It took 58% of the mothers in this study one to three months to conceive, 22% three to six months, and 20%, 6 months or longer.

FERTILITY (BIRTH) RATE: The ratio of the number of births per year to the number of women of child-bearing age.

FREQUENCY OF MULTIPLE BIRTHS: There are approximately 36,000 sets of twins born each year in the United States. Twins occur once in 90 births (once in 73.2 non-white births and once in 93.2 white births). Blacks have the most twins while 1 out of 155 Oriental births result in twins. In Ireland, the rate is 1 in 77 births. Triplets occur about once in 9,300 births: quadruplets once in 490,000 births: quintuplets once in 55,000 births. "Hellin's Law (named for the researcher who formulated it about a century ago) still provides generally accepted prediction abut the frequency of all multiple births. Hellin said that for the human species altogether there would be one twin birth for every 89 single births: that for every 89 twin births there would be one triplet birth: that for every 89 triplet births, one quadruplet birth: and so on up the scale of mathematical changes. Taken from TWINS: *NATURE'S AMAZING MYSTERY* by Kay Cassill.

FRATERNAL/IDENTICAL RATIO: In the United States' white population, there are 65 fraternal twins born for every 35 identical twins. There are 70 fraternal twins born for every 30 identical for American blacks.

TWINNING RATE FOR IDENTICAL (MZ) TWINS: The rate is fairly constant throughout the world and in different races at approximately 4/1000 births: an accident of nature. Chances of having two sets of identical twins is one in 70,000.

TWINNING RATE FOR FRATERNAL (DZ) TWINS: The rate

varies with maternal race, highest in African populations, lowest in Far Eastern populations, and somewhere in between in Europe and the United States. This is thought to be due to alterations in the level of hormones which stimulate the ovary to produce eggs. Other factors that influence the DZ twinning rate is age of mother (white women under twenty have a very low twinning incidence, one in 167 births while women ages 35 to 40 have an incidence of one in 50): number of previously conceived children (a white woman of 35-40) has one chance in 74 of bearing twins her first pregnancy but on her seventh pregnancy the chance increases to one in 45): and by taking drugs to stimulate ovulation. There is also speculation that residency in rural areas, unwed mothers, seasons of the year, and social class have some relationship on the twinning rate.

TWIN TYPING: Method used to determine zygosity or type of twin, ie., identical or fraternal. Placental examination is the most common although it can result in a false diagnosis. The Louisville Twin Study reports that 15 percent of cases reported to have two placentas (fraternal) actually were identical. For example, it is now known that identical twins can have separate placentas and fraternal twins can have fused placentas. As soon as an egg is fertilized, the cells begin to multiply, and are among the earliest formed, and the cells which will become the baby's placenta. If the division into identical twins occurs before these cells have become attached to the wall of the uterus, the twins will have separate placentas (occurring in 25-30 percent of identical pairs). If the division occurs later, the twins will have only one placenta. A microscopic examination is necessary. Additional ways of twin typing are blood examination, fingerprinting and skin grafting.

CONCORDANCE: Term used by researchers meaning in agreement or in accordance, harmonious, same understanding,

25

consensus of opinion, pact, unanimity, compatible.

DISCORDANCE: Term used by researchers meaning in disagreement, unlikeness, dissimilar, incompatible, mismatched, not the same, distinctive, distinguishing.

DIAGNOSIS OF MULTIPLE BIRTH: With the help of medical technology, multiple births are diagnosed earlier than in the past.

One, not-too-recent study, shows that a multiple pregnancy was diagnosed before delivery in less than 705 of the cases. Information taken from NOMOTC's Data Base shows that things are much different today.

LABOR: The fact that twins tend to be smaller than singletons may help to ease their birth. An ordinary plural labor is shorter than an ordinary single labor. Yet there are a greater proportion of sluggish labors because of over distention of the uterus.

INTERVAL BETWEEN BIRTH OF TWINS: The interval between the birth of twins is usually brief. One study reports that 3/4 of all twins are delivered within an hour. Usually five to ten minutes are allowed to elapse before the doctor starts delivery of the second twin.

BIRTH PRESENTATION: In single births, almost 96 percent of babies are born headfirst and 3 1/2 percent are born breech. In multiple births, the situation is quite different. The first twin is usually born head first. The second twin is often breech or crosswise. In less than half of all deliveries are both twins born head first. One study shows that out of every 100 sets of twins, 47 pair will present themselves with both headfirst: 37 pair will both be breech: five pair will have one headfirst and other lying crosswise: and two pair will have one twin breech and the other crosswise. In only one out of 200 cases will both twins be lying crosswise.

The average birth weight of singletons is 71/2 lbs., average birth weight of twins is five lbs. five oz. A difference of two to three pounds in birth weights of twins is not extraordinary.

BIRTH WEIGHT: Identical twins weight becomes more similar as they get older. Usually the degree of similarity at 24 months is maintained at ages three, five, and eight years. Fraternal twins tend to show a decline in weight resemblance from birth to eight years. In boy/girl twins, boys tend to weigh slightly more than twin girls at birth. By the age of 6 months, girl twins weigh an average of one and a half pounds less than their boy co-twin. Boy/girl twins show a marked reduction in weight resemblance during the first year, more similar at 24 months, and less similar at eight years.

BIRTH LENGTH/WEIGHT: Fraternal, same-sex twins, are more similar in length than both identical and boy/girl twins. Yet by age 8 are increasingly different. On the average, at birth, twins are about one inch shorter than singletons. On the average, girls of boy/girl sets are one inch shorter than their boy co-twin and the difference is maintained for two years. Then the girl twins grow more rapidly than boy twins.

FINGERPRINTS: Identical twins are more similar than fraternal twins. Characteristics can be affected by various intrauterine environmental influences. Because males have a larger number of ridges on their fingers, boy/girl twins show a greater difference than same-sex twins.

HAND PREFERENCE: There is a higher incidence of left-handedness in twins compared to singletons. One study showed 22 percentof both identical and fraternal twins are left-handed compared to 11 percent of left-handeders in general population.

SPEECH/LANGUAGE DEVELOPMENT IN TWINS: Twins may be slower (by about three months) than singletons because twins are more frequently premature, often develop their own language, and their mothers have less time to help them develop verbal skills.

27

By the time twins are eight years old, they have usually caught up with singletons.

IDIOGLOSSIA: A condition in which the affected person pronounces his words so badly as to seem to speak a language of his own: Utterance of meaningless sounds. Mothers of twins define it as "twin talk": however, true idioglossia appears to be extremely rare and results when twins are extremely separated from other humans and rely entirely on each other.

SOCIAL DEVELOPMENT IN TWINS: Identical twins develop socially at about the same rate. They tend to show the same degree of competency in dealing with others, usually have similar interest patterns and have similar attitudes and feelings. Fraternal twins differ from each other in social development to almost the same degree as ordinary siblings, especially if they are of different sexes. Environment and parental guidance can have an effect on their children's
similarities and differences.

DEPENDENCE OF TWINS: Girl twins, especially identical, are frequently more dependent than either boy/girl or boy twins. Most likely to remain very close throughout life are identical girls followed by fraternal girls, identical boys, fraternal boys and boy/girl pairs. This is also the order of their dependence on each other.

INTELLIGENCE (IQ) OF TWINS: Identical twins seldom vary more than five points, while the IQs of fraternals may be as different as those for singletons born in the same family. Although, on the average, they are more similar to each other than ordinary brothers and sisters. Twins, on the average, score below the general population. Scores are lower, on the average, for identical twins than
fraternal twins, and lower for fraternal same-sex twins than

28

boy/girl twins.

* * *

CHAPTER III

Companionship And Comparison
In Tandem Lives

More than any other factor, adult twins of all types mention having a "built-in playmate" as a positive aspect of their childhood. Whether or not there are other children in the family, twins never need to spend much time alone. There is always another nearby who is their own age, and who knows them intimately.

A 30-year-old Oregon woman wrote of her relationship with her twin brother: "A positive aspect of having a twin is that we were never alone. Even as infants we did not want for a playmate; we had each other. That feeling has carried through to our adult lives. We remain very close."

Because they are together so much twins have many new experiences at the same time, from their first visit to the dentist to their first day at school. New and frightening events need not be endured alone. Anticipation and excitement can be shared. Moves to new towns or new schools are easier because, as Pooh, the fictional bear, said, "Two can stick together."

A minister in his fifties, who lives in Illinois, told me that having a twin made moving to new neighborhoods easier when he was a child. " Both in being accepted in new schools and having a built-in playmate who did not change with the other changes, made the adjustment easier."

Eighteen -year-old Andrea Johnson, of Hutchinson, Kansas, commented: "I always had someone there who was going through the same thing at the same time and it made it easier to talk to him."

Even when twins are older and their lives have taken different paths, the bond created through shared childhood experiences usually remains strong. Ellen Baron, 40, Malverne, New York, recalled growing up with her twin brother: "We went through so many experiences together. Everything that happened in the world, special events, family situations, music, etc. were experienced by us at the exact same time. The closeness that developed was so special that although we grew up very separately and went forward in different lifestyles, and don't get to see each other too often, that special unspoken feeling will always be there between us."

In childhood, twins rarely know the isolation of the single child, who may have no close peer with whom to share thoughts, feelings, and new life experiences. In any situation, twins can watch and learn from the consequences of each other's behavior. They have the advantage of being able to discuss and compare their reactions to people, situations, and experiences. In dialogues with their twins, their own opinions may be validated, or they may be challenged to look at their views from another angle.

Even when they no longer share constant physical

31

togetherness, many adult twins maintain these patterns of close communication. Richard Pittis, 24, of Edmonds, Washington, said of his relationship with his fraternal twin brother: "What I think stands out now is that anytime we need support, advice, or just someone to shoot the breeze with, we always call each other. We know that the other will drop anything and listen fully to what we say, and best of all will give a truthful feeling back. This confidence in each other helps one in many situations. Two heads are better than one."

Twenty-one-year old Maryanne Danner, of Edmonds, Washington, an identical twin who contributed to my study, spoke for many when she observed: "You have a chance to be a part of someone else's life, as well as your own. To live through them, and they through you."

For a few, the constant presence of their twin can help them survive difficult or traumatic childhood situations. One adult twin told me this story: "My sister and I were adopted by my mother's second husband at age three. He never liked us and let it be known. I was more strong-willed and spoke up, so was punished more. We would receive razor belt spankings for going barefoot in the house, not turning off a light, etc. It took years to get over being put down by him. Positive side, though, is---I really feel I had an inner strength and security with my twin. I feel like a survivor and it feels good."

Apart from such extreme situations, is the "security" of constant togetherness an advantage? Some twins say yes, some say no, depending on their own experiences and memories. Psychologists recognize that individuals grow when encouraged to "stretch" themselves beyond their "comfort zone," and some twins may find it too tempting to remain in the non-challenging safety of their twin's companionship.

For shy, nonassertive twins, it can be comforting to let another be the spokesperson, decision-maker, and initiative-taker in any given situation. Yet they pay a price for remaining in their twin's shadow. Adult twins of all types expressed regret at not having learned, as children, to assert their own thoughts and feelings and preferences, or to exercise leadership at least some of the time. One woman wrote: "It is only in later years that I have learned to stand on my own two feet and express my own ideas, for I always let my twin take the lead in whatever we did."

Wrote a fraternal twin woman in her mid-fifties, "I appeared very confident and was quite a participant in college after I left my twin. As matrons our roles are almost reversed. To me, my twin is much more confident and outgoing than I. As an adult I have mostly accepted my role of being not very special."

Twins rarely have to---or are allowed to---amuse themselves or spend much time in solitary introspection. Some twins consequently find it difficult and uncomfortable to be alone. Some are paralyzed when called upon to make autonomous decisions. One member of a male-female pair, in her early forties, confided the following to me: "Very recently I found myself involved in situations where I opted for partnerships when I should have gone it alone. I wondered if that was because I had grown up as part of a pair and had been very comfortable with that set-up; thereby not being comfortable at the prospect of taking full responsibility even though I felt capable of doing so."

In my study, adult twins often regretted that their closeness with their twin prevented them from developing deep relationships with parents, other siblings, or outside friends. A 29-year-old identical said: "Having a twin gives you a best friend, someone who knows you better than anyone else ever will. This can be great, but it can also cause problems. I can't open myself up to my own friends now as much as they can with me. I may talk over problems with friends, but I won't shed tears in front of them. I'd do that with my sister."

It is not surprising that twins often fail to reproduce the deeply-rewarding childhood intimacy of twinship in their adult relationships. No other person could possibly match the closeness of nine months spent together "in utero", shared birthdays, shared growing experiences, and even---for some---a shared private language. Researchers estimate that close to 40 percent of all twins---identical and fraternal---develop a language of their own during early childhood. The scientific term for this phenomenom is "idioglossia." A California woman recalled communicating in secret words with her identical twin sister: "When we were very small we had our "own" language. No one else could understand us."

Twin babble has been identified in many cases with complete sentences that have the syntax, qualifiers and modifiers necessary to make the speech intelligible to the twins spouting it.

"Booley-Hookie-Wally-Hankie."

These were the words invented by twins meaning, "Comfort me." I learned them from two grown women at a Labor Day twins convention. They explained they remembered them from their childhood together.

"Henny-Google," was their substitute for the expression, "I am embarrassed."

Idiolglossia demonstrates the inventiveness of twins who share a unique world of their own, and whether they speak in a secret language or not, they often baffle outsiders who marvel at the ability of one twin to complete a sentence the other has started with no hesitation. It seems quite obvious that sharing on all the levels that twins do, from looking and dressing alike, to thinking, acting, and playing alike, creates a remarkable interdependent relationship between them.

Idioglossia can be used to exclude other people, and it may continue to affect twins' adult communication patterns, as one 57-year-old identical woman recognized: "We had our own language and I am sure our mother and father felt left out. Also, so many times when the two of us are talking we do not have to complete our sentences. I find that I even do this when talking to other people."

Some researchers believe that twins' private communication patterns, both verbal and non-verbal, may be the reason twins in general seem to develop language skills somewhat later than singletons. As twins grow older and interact more with others, their private language is lost. One 38-year-old fraternal man recalled: "We had our own language when we were very young. I cannot remember it, but would be very interested in being able to hear what it sounded like."

I had the opportunity to observe this private twin language while visiting my own grandsons shortly after they began to talk. The guest bedroom was next to their nursery. Often I would be awakened by fast chatter, followed by much laughter. During the day, I would listen to them communicate as they played, but I was never able to understand a word.

I would like to know if my sister and I, or my older twin brothers, ever had a language of our own. I have no recollection of such a thing, and my parents never made mention of it.

Sharing of language, of experiences, of thoughts and feelings is an oft-mentioned aspect of growing up with the constant companionship of a twin. This includes the sharing of THINGS, as well. A 59-year-old California identical wrote: " I recall eating only half a piece of candy and saving the other for her, as she did for me. One piece of gum had to be chewed five minutes by each in turn!"

Single children rarely have to deal with relatives who give one holiday gift and expect two children to share it, a situation twins frequently encounter. Some of my survey respondents recalled their early, enforced lessons in sharing as a long-range benefit; others described deep resentment over having few if any childhood possessions to call their own.

Twinship also means sharing attention---from parents and from others. This may be a case where single children have an advantage, for every single-born child gets to be the "baby of the family" for some period of time after birth. Twins never do; from the time they enter the world, they must learn to wait their turn to be fed, diapered, and cuddled. They learn to wait to describe their day at school, or to start down the playground slide. Even though twins receive a good deal of attention that singletons never experience, just because of the fact that they are twins, it is not individual attention. This may contribute to the difficulty twins often have in establishing a firm sense of individual identity.

"Know thyself---human beings have received this advice throughout recorded time, from Biblical sages, philosophers, mystics, and modern psychotherapists. It is a lifelong task for all thoughtful individuals who seek to discover the essence of themselves, and to decide how they fit into the great human collective we call "society."

This process is complicated enough for single-born individuals who must define themselves separately from parents, siblings, peer groups, and authority figures. Besides all these, twins have a powerful added dimension to deal with---the need to establish a sense of self separate from the person with whom they were conceived, entered the world, and have spent most of their lives---a

36

person with whom they have frequently been identified as part of a unit, a pair---"The Twins."

The single child asks "Who am I?" The twin says "We are twins, but who am I?"

Most individuals draw much of their self-concept and self-esteem from how other people react to them. For twins, this can be very confusing, for other people frequently respond to them more as a pair than as individuals. As one identical woman cryptically described the dilemma of the twin in the eyes of the world: "You will never be more than one, but you will never be less than two."

Why does this matter? Why is it so important for twins to know themselves as individuals, apart from their twin? For that matter, what is anyone looking for in the search to "know thyself?"

Some of the best-selling books in the last decade have been those which help people find insights into who they are, as individuals. Everyone is looking for direction on how to get more out of life---how to reach their full potential, make a contribution, and realize the greatest joy that is possible. In other words, we are asking: "How can I be happy and fulfilled, and feel that my life has meaning?"

To be autonomous, to know and accept one's thoughts and feelings, to have peace of mind---in other words, to be content---is the goal of all individuals, whether or not they are consciously aware of it.

For a few twins, mostly identicals, a self-identity as half of a pair is all they desire. But since even identical twins are not clones (something other people too often forget), most twins want to be known and valued---as themselves and by others---as unique, special, and worthwhile individuals who also happen to be twins. The more alike twins are in appearance, tastes, aptitudes and abilities, the more difficult it is for each to establish a separate sense of self and a strong individual self-esteem.

What are the characteristics of this "strong individual self-esteem" that is so important to human fulfillment and contentment? Psychologist Nathaniel Branden, in his book *Honoring The Self* , defines self-esteem as "the experience that one is competent to live and worthy of happiness."

"Competence to live is the knowledge that you are able to maintain your life through the ability to learn and to take effective action. It is the deeply-held belief that you can function appropriately without undue dependence on anyone or anything outside yourself. 'Worthiness' is knowing that your life has meaning, that you are important, and you deserve to be happy. The two components are interdependent. A sense of competence increases your sense of worthiness, and the feeling of worthiness motivates efforts to increase your area of competence."

For twins, more than single children, the issue of dependence/ independence is pivotal to their search for individual self-esteem. Many of the "benefits" of constant companionship chronicled earlier in this chapter have a strong tendency to foster dependency---sometimes for one twin, sometimes for both---and to discourage the development of individual self-reliance.

Twins' confusion about their identity often starts at a very young age. Dr. Janet W. Kizziar and Dr. Judy W. Hagedorn, psychologists and authors of *Gemini: The Psychology and Phenomena Of Twins* , discovered that the majority of preschool and primary grade twins believed such ideas as:

*One twin was the "real" person, and the other only a shadow.

*They were the same person split in two.

*They were (or should be) exactly alike in all ways.

Disturbed by these misconceptions, Kizziar and Hagedorn, themselves identical mirror twins, went on to write a children's book,

What Is A Twin, to help young twins avoid these potentially destructive beliefs and the resulting emotional difficulties which they say "often accompany twinship."

In simple language, their book addresses issues which all twins encounter and which can indeed contribute to twins' difficulties in developing strong individual identities and self-esteem. One of the most universal issues for twins is that of labeling.

A fraternal twin living in Bothell, Washington, expressed his frustration with labeling. "We were always called 'The Twins.' That drove me nuts. We are no where near the same people. When I hear people saying, 'The Twins,' I feel like they think we are identical, the same personalities, etc. We aren't! We are totally different!"

All twins---identical and fraternal---often find themselves labeled "The Twins" instead of being called by their individual names. The subtle message each twin may hear is: "You don't count by yourself---you are only half of an indistinguishable pair."

Identical twins encounter this type of labeling more frequently than fraternals. People use it out of laziness, or to cover their inability to tell the twins apart. Amazing as it may seem, even parents sometimes "take the easy way out" and call their twin children "twins" or "twinnies" or a hyphenated combination of their two given names. More that one respondent in my survey told me he thought his name was "Ed-n-Gene" or "Don-John" for his first few years of life.

In an attempt to be clever, parents of twins often give their children rhyming names, names that are similar in spelling, or names of couples from history or literature. Male-female twins, in particular, sometimes have to deal with embarrassing attention because of names like Jack and Jill, even Mary and Joseph.

39

Labeling of children by their dominant characteristics occurs within many families, but it happens more often to twins. Sometimes parents do it quite innocently in an attempt to distinguish one from the other. Some respondents mentioned often hearing their parents say things like, "This is my swimmer," or "This is my reader" when introducing the twins to other people.

The only problem with such descriptive tags is when the children's self-images become limited by the labels. If one twin is called "The Reader," the other may not pursue a love of reading. If one is labeled "The Athlete" and the other "The Student", each may be discouraged from developing a well-rounded personality that includes both athletic and academic interests.

Labeling becomes really destructive when it implies an "either-or" value judgment, and unfortunately people tend to use these labels often and insensitively in regard to twins. Many twins quoted elsewhere in this book wrote of the pain and self-doubts they experienced from being labeled "the Good One", or "the Smart One", also suffered from the comparative labels, as they saw their twin's pain and as they realized that a label could just as easily be reversed.

Even when the labels imply no value judgment, twins quickly pick up on which characteristic is more approved. "The Shy One" is not likely to feel as adequate or competent as "the Outgoing One". Because people tend to choose labels which imply opposites, twins who are really not very far apart on a given trait may hardly recognize themselves in others descriptions. For example, "the Tall One" may only stand an inch taller that her sister, or "the Fat One" may really be of average weight but merely a little bit heavier that her/his twin. Yet these labels may affect individual twins' self-image and self-esteem well into adulthood and indeed for the rest of their lives.

Nicknames given by parents and others can have destructive or limiting effects on both singletons and twins, but twins may be more adversely affected by them because of twins' already-less-secure identities. One twin was a tomboy whose father called her "Slats" because of her skinny legs; she said she hated it, and it contributed to a long-lasting difficulty in accepting herself as an attractive woman.

Most children, including twins, derive a large part of their self-image from the way other people respond to them, as do adults. Labels too often tend to become self-fulfilling prophesies which can limit an individual's growth as a well-rounded, whole human being. Whether twins are "lumped together" as a unit or distinguished from each other by labels, their individual identities are too often molded by the names others call them.

Surprisingly, even twins get labeled "the Older" and "the Younger." as are most singletons who are not "only" children. This distinction may seem ridiculous when applied to twins, yet it had a profound effect on a surprising number of my respondents. Several wrote bitterly of having never been allowed to forget that they were the last-born, even if it was by only a few minutes. The "older" twin would "pull rank" on the younger, and parents often went along with them in assigning privileges or allowing decision-making priority.

Birth order even affects how parents feel about their twins. In an article for Twins Magazine, Elinor Davis quoted research on twins' birth order at Australia's La Trobe University. It was found that "...both parents generally "feel closer" to the first born and perceive the first twin as "easier to manage, less fussy, and healthier." A twin study in Louisville, also quoted by Davis, showed that "...secondborns had more feeding and "temper" problems, but fewer sleeping problems. However, the secondborns were also reported as laughing and smiling more readily, coinciding with the

La Trobe finding that secondborns were rated by parents as "more affectionate."

Much research has shown that birth order is an important factor in all individuals' development of personal identity. Obviously, many additional factors within the family affect a twin's emerging self-image: number, sex and spacing of siblings; where the twins fit into the overall birth sequence; parents' socioeconomic and educational status; parents' own place in their birth order and how it affects their treatment of their children. Each individual personality is a unique combination of genes, experiences, and relationships. Twins, because of the "accident" of sharing their birthday, have many experiences that single children never encounter.

Identical and fraternal twins experience different effects of having more attention focused on their twinship than on their individuality. Fraternal twins, who may look no more alike than any pair of siblings, sometimes have a hard time convincing others that they are in fact twins. When this very basic fact of their existence is questioned, and when doubt is simultaneously cast upon their truthfulness, it is not surprising that fraternal twins may have problems feeling good about themselves---as individuals or as twins.

A fraternal twin living in Roswell, New Mexicao reported, "Because my twin and I are so different especially in looks and personality, I never thought much about being a twin. People who met us never believed we were twins, as we would make up stories about one of us being adopted."

Identical twins never have to convince anyone of their twinship, but they may have to convince others of which one they are. If they are dressed alike as children, if their hair styles and personal mannerisms are very similar (as they often are), and if they are frequently called by their twin's name by people who can't tell them apart, then it's no wonder that identical twins may ask themselves: "Who am I, really?"

Twins' confusion can be increased by well-meaning others who, not wanting to appear to "show favoritism", treat the two children exactly alike. While recognizing twins' individual differences and treating them accordingly does run the risk of appearing "unequal", many twins reported preferring that over being treated like clones.

One of the common misconceptions young twins have about themselves, according to Drs. Kizziar and Hagedorn, is the idea that they are (or should be) exactly alike in all ways. This idea is too often reinforced by adults who believe the same thing. People who send mixed messages that twins should be exactly alike, and then proceed to point out their differences, undermine twins' individual self-esteem and drive a wedge between them. The results are often feelings of competition, jealousy, and resentment on the part of one or both twins. Such feelings, which foster defensiveness rather that openness, can prevent the twins from knowing each other deeply as individuals.

One 31-year-old identical wrote of mixed feelings despite her close childhood relationship with her twin: "I wish there were some way to explain to people what it's like---mere words can't explain the feelings---love, hate, tenderness, sympathy, jealousy, etc." Separated since her twin's marriage at age 19, she later realized: "I truly regret having taken "being a twin" for granted. Not getting to know her as a person---how she fells about certain things, you know. Just getting together alone, like a retreat, to re-know each other---after 12 years of separation and growing, separately, it truly would be fun to do!"

Almost all siblings are compared to one another to some degree, but twins are compared far more often, because of the very natural need to distinguish between them. As shown earlier when discussing labels, innocently-intended comparisons too often imply value judgments and have a negative effect on the twins' self-image.

The twins in my survey felt they were most often compared physically and intellectually/academically. Most disliked being compared, and felt that it diminished them as individuals. One twin said: "I never understood it as a child, and as an adult I still don't understand why anyone would ever compare one person with another, for each of us is a unique and individual person."

Another twin said: "I think for anyone to compare one person against another is cruel."

Fraternal twins may suffer from comparisons that would never be made if they were not known to be twins. L.M.S., a 52-year-old Everett, Washington fraternal female wrote: "My twin sister and I do not resemble each other physically or in personality. Growing up, we were subjected to adult comments, and heard My, one is short and fat, the other tall and thin, or look at that. One is blond, the other dark. As little children we were very shy, and I think that was a contributing factor."

Though physical differences cannot be disguised, twins may try to de-emphasize their individual interests and stifle any growth in separate directions, to avoid the discomfort of comparisons. One articulate example comes from a Washington woman who grew up in a large family which included three sets of twins. She described her adult relationship with her twin as "very good," but she remembers vividly the dilemma created by her own expectation that twins must always be alike: "I've thought, at times, how my life might have been different. I believe we often did things together at an older age because there existed a feeling that we should like similar things. For that same reason, there were activities that neither one of us tried, probably because our roles were fairly well defined, and though we explored further areas, we stayed pretty close within those roles. This found one or the other not trying in that area since we didn't want to play one against the other. Here you see where comparison as well as competition enters the picture. One instance where I was able to explore what it was like to create an image outside of my twin role and its overriding influence was when I attended a different high school. I was able to try activities I'd been hesitant to try before. I turned out for tennis, the first sport I'd done without my twin following suit. It was great. I am grateful for that opportunity because it helped me visualize myself as an individual outside my twin."

Ironically, when twins pursue their separate interests, to avoid competition and comparison, they may end up resenting each other more. Having to sacrifice the self for the twinship may cause guilt feelings and anger for not being more alike or feeling more loving toward each other. For these twins, separation may be painful, but it may also mean liberation; at last, to "find themselves" as individuals.

One twin, by flip of a coin, won the opportunity to spend a year overseas, without his brother. He wrote that it was a wonderful way to learn to see himself as a totally separate individual.

Expectations of alikeness and comparisons of differences created some bizarre and contradictory reactions in the twins I surveyed. Whereas some twins submerged their individuality to keep peace within the twinship, a few others felt the need to act and be different from their twin just to have a sense of themselves as individuals, even if, in fact, they were very like their twin in may ways.

The common result was this: any time individuals submerged their own natural interests and traits, whether these were similar to or different from their twin's, both their individual self-esteem and their feelings of closeness to their twin were diminished.

Twins get attention---lots of it---just for being two. Unlike singletons, they don't have to do anything special to earn the attention they get; they don't have to be beautiful, or talented, or virtuous. This can be "good news", when it helps twins develop social self-confidence, or it can be "bad news", when twins get the message that they needn't develop any special skills or accomplishments to get attention. As Drs, Kizziar and Hagedorn have noted: "Few twins are high achievers."

Twins are never at a loss for something to talk about when meeting strangers, for it seems like everyone is fascinated with the question "What's it like to be a twin?"

A 28-year-old Montana woman with a twin brother wrote that being twins "meant receiving special attention whenever we were introduced to someone new in the community, at school, at church, etc. As a child I certainly enjoyed the attention; even now it's something to talk about, like the weather, when meeting new people."

Andrea Johnson, 18, from Hutchinson, Kansas, recalled that she and her brother "got put in the paper, on the front page, last year because we were twins and the last of 10 children graduating."

"We were always in the limelight," said many twins. Some enjoyed the extra attention, yet others were embarrassed or uncomfortable in the spotlight. Several of my respondents who work in show business or in the ministry speculated that their early experiences as the center of attention may have influenced them to choose professions which put them in the public eye.

Not all attention twins receive is positive, as my fraternal twin respondents often recalled with pain. If attention called to their twinship meant comparisons and feelings of inadequacy, they would rather not have had it.

A few twins wrote that, as adults, they now realize that their singleton siblings were often not given as much attention as they received as twins, and they felt badly about having been the reason their siblings were slighted.

Outside the family, the spotlight on the twins is usually equally shared. Within the family, if one gets more attention, for whatever reason (parental favoritism, or one twin's health), the effect on the "less-favored twin" can be very painful. Several twins mentioned that their twin was often sickly as a child, and thus received more parental attention. As adults, the "healthier" twins recognized that this was only natural, yet as children they often felt "left out" or "less loved."

It seems fitting to close this chapter with a thoughtful essay on the lifetime experience of being identical twin girls, as written by Karen Riley of Sleepy Hollow, Illinois. It expresses the strong unity that characterizes the struggle for identity in many twinships:

"We were two peas in a pod, Ike and Mike, the look alikes, the dynamic duo, double the pleasure, double the fun. This sense of confidence and power was magnified by dressing alike. I suppose we felt there was nothing we couldn't face together.

Our bond of bravado and loyalty was woven into many experiences from early life well into early adulthood. I know it was some of our shared histories that kept us close and faithful to one another.

When we were toddlers, the milkman was accused of not leaving the weekly order of butter. Weeks later, buried in our toy chest, mom found the rancid butter. Rather than squeal, we would defiantly remain silent and take any punishment together.

In our teen years, this sense of justice was kept strong in other areas of our life. We would share a paycheck until the other found a summer job. When one twin lay all the groundwork of flirting with a boy at school and he asked the other one out by mistake, the whole incident was taken graciously and the victim bowed out with dignity.

In college, our twin-individuality became very apparent. Career paths became distinctively different; one going into nursing and the other into art and journalism. In the past, we would have taken turns encouraging each other through crises. Suddenly, our system became unreliable and unbalanced as one twin's life became more out of control. It was a year of misunderstandings.

In adulthood, this pattern continued with multiple pregancy losses, slowly developing alcholism and financial problems. Was it the inability of the other twin to deal with the pain or just helplessness? Perhaps it was a realization that this was something we couldn't face together. Nevertheless, the gulf widened.

In recent reflection, we can comprehend that it was those very stresses that we weren't able to share that made our paths divergent and unique. I know it was a necessary good. Our sameness brought security. It was the differences that would shape our unique selves and allow us to be loyal to our own emerging identities. It was our differences that would bring us back to each other in a healthy way.

I think we struggle with our separateness; the "we" versus the "1". It is almost as if we both can't be right if we don't share the sameness. To have different opinions, like experiences or feelings would make us less of a "we". Instinctively, the more separate "we" become, the more "we" we are. It makes us able to become---not half to another half but a whole to a whole. The bonding becomes stronger with time and the confidence and loyalty are one again. But this time we come as two wonderfully unique pea pods, not just two peas in a pod."

CHAPTER IV

Parents Set The Stage

In her book, *Since You Asked Me*, Columnist Ann Landers made a statement about twins that should be of interest to every parent of twins. She said every twin should adopt the motto: "One thing I can do better than anybody else is to be myself."

Such a motto reflects the attitude parents must adopt to shape the individual development of their twins. For more than any other influence, it is the parents who set the stage for how their twin children are going to perceive themselves and how they are going to be viewed by others.

Children grow at their own pace. It is the job of the parents to observe their twins and let each develop at his own speed. The depth of the parental stewardship imprint on twins can be gauged by the comments of adult twins who have grown to maturity with designs for living that have been set soundly in place.

One twin, in her mid-fifties, Mrs. N.B. wrote: "I was never alone. I grew up with my twin, married for 30 years. Then my husband passed away. I was desolated, alone for the first time in my life. I had to learn to be with myself. The first few years after his death I grew up. Living alone was very hard but now I'm OK and getting on with life."

Another twin in her middle years is still bitter over the favoritism shown to her twin sister by her parents.

"I have had a lot of feelings about my relationship with my parents ever since I was young and I realized I would have to spend the rest of my life trying to be as good as my twin was and as important to them as she."

The "preferred" twin has lived with the guilt of being the one her parents liked best, the one whom they held up as a model to their other twin daughter.

The favored twin confessed to me that she was aware of the damage being done to her sister because of the show of partiality, yet felt powerless to do anything about it. She also felt that her mother's unfair treatment of her sister resulted in the sister developing an inferiority complex and bitterness toward her mother and her sister.

Another twin told me: "We lived on a farm and my twin sister loved driving the tractor. I liked housework, baking and cooking, so in my father's eyes I wasn't much good to him. He made it very obvious that my sister was the favored one."

On the opposite end of the scale are twins who are inseparable emotionally and psychologically. They function best when they are together. Parents must make the difficult decision at an early stage of whether to encourage individuality or allow a happy situation to continue.

As an example, I know two concert pianists, Clarice and Alice Rainer of Winston-Salem, North Carolina. They enjoy sharing every facet of their lives together. Their pink poodles accompany them when they go on concert tours. "We have dressed exactly alike," they told me, "for all of our 57 years and we would not have it any other way. We even make sure, for example, that in a floral print dress or blouse, the same flower is in the same place in each outfit."

Little children are quite perceptive and take all manners of clues from their parents as to how they are perceived by them and the adult world. One of the subtle ways parents use to distinguish between identical twins, often unconsciously, is the birth order of the children. The one born first often is perceived to be less fussy, healthier, and dominant.

Some interesting studies have been done in birth order, but up to this time, no physiological basis has been discovered for the assertion of leadership or dominant qualities in the twin who arrives first.

The writer Elinor Davis tells about a set of fraternal twin men who reported that they were fascinated as to which of them was first and second born and they concocted a fantasy about their life in the womb. They imagined they were millionaires getting ready for a ball but they were already late. One twin said his brother forgot his cane and went back to get it. That's why Mike was born first and his twin, who had forgotten his cane, was born second.

It is a well known fact that the survival rate of the first born twin is greater than that of the second born twin. That fact seems to argue for being born first if there were such a thing as choice in the matter.

Some twins have so exaggerated the importance of birth order that tragedy had resulted.

This was the case of Todd and Timothy Nicholson, heirs to the Pullman Car and Cudahy Meat Packing fortunes. Deprived of their father early and raised by a quarrelsome, embittered mother, the

51

boys lacked a sense of security and identity. Todd, the oldest by two minutes, would pistol-whip Timothy in a rage to prove he was superior. Finally, Timothy rebelled and shot Todd to death. After his release from prison, Timothy married his brother's fiance who faithfully visited him while he was confined.

Perhaps the biggest difference between how twins are raised compared to single children is how they are perceived by their family. If parents of twins would always realize they are raising two children, not two lookalikes with the same personality, it would lessen the unreal expectations that are so often placed upon twins.

I've often been asked what twins feel are the most positive and negative aspects of twinship? My answer, based on talking with hundreds of twins, is that on the positive side, there is the built-in playmate. On the negative, the comparisons parents make between them. Out of parental comparisons come expectations which result in a host of feelings, mostly destructive ones. I touched lightly on the problem of comparisons in the previous chapter; here, we explore the harm they can do.

Typical of destructive feeling is one expressed by the woman who said her twin sister was always stronger-willed than she, but that she felt she was more attractive. "We were always being compared, even to this day," she said.

Comparisons can leave deep scars, as this moving statement from a woman in her late twenties indicates:

"During certain periods of my life I felt I paled in comparison to my twin in physical attractiveness and social popularity. The physical difference was in part due to a club foot I was born with. My twin did not have to deal with being handicapped. This had a bearing on our being compared as twins. Later in life, I grew into an attractive person and this favorably evened things out. It is painful to be compared to a sibling when one clearly has the advantage over the other. My twin was a cheerleader, I was not, although I was better in sports and later became Girl of the Year and Prom Queen."

Comparison can be devastating and harmful to anyone, but it seems to be never-ending for twins who are very different in most all ways.

One 30 year old twin I know put in perspective for all twins the problem of comparison:

"Being a twin, people like to compare your different traits, likes, dislikes, looks. I felt I wanted my independence from comparison. To be looked at for myself."

Many of the twins I came to know feel the sting of comparison, but also realize that it is their twinship that caused them to be so often compared. One twin observed: "It is hard as a twin and a parent of twins, not to compare twins. I was fortunate in that my parents allowed my brother and me to go our separate ways as far as development, as I would think in most twin cases the two personalities would develop quite differently."

Height, weight and coloring are areas where fraternal twins are often quite different. Unfortunately, these are also areas where culturally-accepted ideals of beauty come into play, especially for girls and women.

For example, one twin may be petite and fine-featured while the other may have a large bone structure. One may be prone to obesity while the other is of average weight. Such discrepancies can cause much distress among twins, because of the value our culture currently puts on delicacy and slenderness as marks of attractiveness in women. Twins internalize cultural "ideals" as do other girls, but the "less-favored" twin may suffer more than a single child with the same attributes, because the twin has a built-in "standard" for comparison---her own twin sister. One twin told of being devastated by unfair comparisons to her twin:

"I remember," she said, "feeling insecure about being compared, and I think it increased the competition between my twin and me. I felt that anything I accomplished would generalize over to her, thereby taking away some of the 'glory'. Conversely, if she did something wrong, it would generalize over to me, too. I felt that we were perceived as a 'unit,' rather than as two people. It wasn't until later in life, when I was alone without my twin, that I felt most insecure, because I couldn't lean on her accomplishments, her advice, her positive 'strokes' and feedback. I think my parents thought of my twin as 'the good twin,' because she didn't cause the problems that I did. My twin always followed directions, listened to our parents, etc. whereas I would rebel. Ironically, I guess I rebelled partly because I wanted their attention and their recognition of me as an individual person who was different."

The number and type of differences between any two female or male twins can mix the blessings of twinship with a good deal of agony, depending on how strangers, friends, and "significant others" react to their individual characteristics, whether in appearance or in personality. In the area of physical appearance, comparisons frequently carry value judgements, and these may deeply affect the individual's sense of attractiveness and acceptability as a person. In extreme cases, a very sensitive child may interpret even seemingly neutral comments about differences as evidence of personal unworthiness. The effect on the child's sense of identity may be something like this: "I'm not what I think I am; I'm not what YOU THINK I am; I am what I THINK you think I am."

Unfair parental comparisons can create competition between twins that can deepen the gulf of rivalry.

Competition between twins can be one of the most effective ways to drive a wedge between children and it can continue into their adult lives. Competition between twin children can serve as a motivator and can be healthy if handled correctly, but it takes a wise, listening parent to accomplish this. Anger is the signal to any parent when competition becomes unhealthy and it is then that parents need to intervene and re-direct the activity of their twins.

For young twins, competition for the attention and love of parents seems to surface most often. Parents need to be especially careful not to show favoritism, for youngsters are always looking for signs of approval from their parents, and are remarkably aware when it seems to be one sided, or not equally given.

Lynn, an identical twin woman in her late twenties addressed the devisiveness that can develop between twins when they have to compete for love.

"I am an extremely competitive person. I honestly believe that it is because all my life I had to compete with my twin for everything from Mom and Dad's love and attention to the attention of some boy. It seems a way of life now."

"It's very hard," she said, "to compete with someone who, to others, is a xerox copy of yourself. On the surface you are competing with another person who looks and sounds just like you. It's just like competing with yourself!"

This woman was convinced that competition can pull twins apart. Parents should be wary of condoning competition if it seems to dominate the relationship between their twins.

To a much greater extent than parents of single children, parents of twins are responsible for the intellectual development of their children. This important contribution by parents was put into focus in a study of 92 twins and 44 single boys by researchers at the University of Calgary.

The findings showed that the non-twin boys were consistently better in performance that the twin boys.

According to Hugh Lytton, Dorice Conway and Reginold Suave of the research team, "It is the parent's reduced speech that contributes to the twins lower verbal facility, rather than a lower facility evoking lesser parent response.

"It's generally a question of the parents of the twins being much more harassed," they say. "At the same time, twins form a coherent unit, giving the impression that they do not need as much attention as many other children."

The most important difference between parents of twins and parents of single children in the University of Calgary study was that the mothers and fathers of non-twins simply spoke more to their children than twin parents did to theirs.

Parents of single-born children also engaged in more control behavior generally. They used more commands and prohibitions, more reasoning and more suggestions, and the mothers were more consistent in enforcing the rules they had laid down. Also parents of non-twins demonstrated more affection toward their youngsters and displayed more "positive action."

Parents of identical twins should not be convinced because of the closeness and interdependence of their twins that the children need them less to contribute to their development. If anything, identical twins need their parents more if they are to grow into intelligent humans with the wisdom to make individual choices. The challenge is for parents to penetrate the bond that similarity creates between the twins, and in such a fashion that the psychological requirements of each child become exposed.

Hard to believe, but true, is the singular question often asked of twins: "Which one of you is smarter?"

Identical twins are less likely to feel hurt responding to such a callous question since they look and often think alike. It can be especially painful for fraternal twins who may be much more discordant.

I. Q. in twins has been researched for many years. Fascinating studies have been done world-wide on this subject. During the early part of the 20th Century, Dr. H.H. Newman, of the University of Chicago, was well known for his extensive research of twins. A twin himself, he reported on an interesting pair of identical twin girls who, when cramming for exams would divide their texts between themselves and each studied one half of the books. Their test scores consistently revealed that they had absorbed the facts from all of the books, even though each had crammed from only one half of them.

Because of the genetic structure of identical twins, they are more likely to score equally in tests than fraternals. My own research has shown that it is the fraternals who have a problem of dealing with disparity in grade accomplishment. It would not be a big issue if each of them was evaluated on an individual basis, and not expected to perform as their twin. The problem arises when grade cards are evaluated in the presence of both twins and comparisons are made.

The latest research on twins and their I.Q.s shows that identical twins seldom vary more than five points while the I.Q.s of fraternals may be as different as those of singletons born in the same family. Twins, on the average, score below the general population. Scores are lower for identical twins than fraternal twins. Part of the reason the lower scoring of identical twins may be attributed to the deprivation of parental talking and emotional conditioning which was noted in the University of Calgary study. This was put in focus by an identical woman who told me: "My parents, for the most part, didn't do a very good job supporting me in my adolescent years as I sought my own identity apart from my twin. I think most of their failure was out of simple ignorance. They didn't develop distinct realationship with either one of us, especially my mother. She assumed that we had each other and could take care of each other when confronting the difficult problems."

It cannot be overemphasized the major role parents have in shaping the future of their twins. It is a far greater influence, if it could be measured on a one-to-one basis, than the impact they have on the single children in the family. Dealing with one child does not seem to carry the weighty responsibility that falls to the parents of twins, especially identicals. Here are two children who look alike, appear to think alike, fall ill of the same ailments, have identical appetites for the same kind of food, and often share a mysterious language understandable to no one but them, and inexperienced parents are asked to cultivate individuality in each of the twins. Teach them to be distinct human beings, parents are urged, and start the process when they are babies with consideration of how they are dressed.

The sure fire way for parents of twins to catch the attention of everyone they meet is to push a stroller that is double in size, double in bodies, and double in wearing apparel. "Aren't they cute?" Of course they are, but should twins be dressed alike? And if so, for how long? Anyone fortunate enough to have had twins has faced these questions.

Judy Morris, who lives in southern Oregon tells of the time her twin sister got mud on her skirt. The girls arranged to call home from school to ask their mother to bring clean clothes. When she arrived she had brought one pair of grey flannel pants to replace a dirty grey flannel skirt. The twins were so upset that they would have to dress differently that it took another trip for their mother to bring the second pair of matching flannel pants.

Aside from the fact that dressing alike can diminish the feeling of uniqueness in twins, it robs each of the twin children of the opportunity to make decisions for themselves about what they want to wear. While it is true that identical twins are more likely to agree upon what "they" wear, there are some identicals who do not share the same likes and styles of clothing and it can be a troubling time for both of them. Some identicals who feel they want to dress alike take turns deciding what they are both going to wear that day.

Some parents admit that they have gone to great lengths to see that their twin children are identical in dress. Such was the extreme action of a mother of identical twins, one of whom reported, "We were groomed to look exactly alike. One time I lost a front tooth. Mother wiggled my twin's tooth until it also came out."

There are many adult twins who say it never occurred to them to dress differently when they were going out.

One twin, a man in his mid-20s, said that when he and his brother were little their parents dressed them alike. One day he asked them why they always had to dress the same. The answer was: "Because you are twins." To which the child replied, "If we always have to dress alike, then I don't want to be a twin anymore."

The issue of dressing alike has quite different significance for fraternal twins than for identicals. For identical twins, matching clothing only underscores an already apparent resemblance (and may make it even harder for other people to tell them apart). For fraternal twins, it may be the first and only advertisement that the two are twins.

Most parents spend a great amount of time pondering what name to give their child. Parents of twins have an even more difficult time since they must come up with two names. As I indicated earlier, parents can be foolish when it comes to naming twins. Lucky for twins---it appears that parents are not giving rhyming names to their twin children as much as they did a few years ago. In my own case, my parents were busy taking care of their first born, twin boys while they were waiting for me to arrive.

Little did they know that I was going to be double. They had chosen the name Betty Louise, and had to scramble fast when they were asked to come up with another name. The final decision was Betty Jean and Fay Louise, giving my twin the first name of our Mother. It is interesting that she is the one who closely resembled Mother while I inherited the facial features of my Father.

When people who are introduced to twins who look alike and who also have similar sounding names, it only makes it more difficult to attach the right name to the right person. Most people like to address a person with his name when they are talking to him, but with twins they may be less likely to do so for fear of using the wrong name.

It is interesting to note that parents of identical twins are more likely to give their children rhyming names than are the parents of fraternal twins. One girl who has a twin brother says she will always be grateful to her grandmother who talked her mother out of naming them Jack and Jill.

Rhyming names not only add to more confusion, but discourage the individuality of the twin children. Here are some of them: Earl/Merle, Roy/Troy, Irwin/Mervin, Cody/Dody, Alena/Colena.

Lindsay Cunningham who has a twin brother remarked that, "Our parents did not compare us with each other, but other relatives always expected the same from us, and a lot of cousins called us Lindsay-Lowell, like our names were one long name."

Twins who are given rhyming names often complain that they find themselves answering to the other's name since they are not sure which name was spoken.

Twins are born with a built-in playmate. They share toys, thoughts, experiences, sentences, and often a bed. But the comfort of always having that security can result in trauma when the security blanket slips off.

Wise are the parents who recognize the need for each of their children to have time to experience life apart from their twin. The earlier these experiences begin, the easier it will be---when the time comes---for them to take divergent paths.

It is a good idea for parents to plan activities for their twins which involve their separation. Such planning will aid in the development of maturity and independence.

Parents should encourage separations and periods of individual reflection for their twins because otherwise:

1. Feelings of interdependence may last a lifetime if the children do not learn to act on their own.
2. The time will come when they will be challenged to know who they are, apart from their twin. Decisions will have to be made independent of the look alike.

The following bit of verse, author unknown, perhaps expresses the dilemma that parents face in the challenging process of raising twins. The message is one that all parents of twins should put in a prominent place as a reminder of their responsibility as custodians of the uniqueness of their twins.

If I am I because of You,
And You are You because of Me;
Then I'm not I, and You're not You.

But if I am I because of Me,
And You are You because of You;
Then I am I and You are You.

CHAPTER V

School Days

It is a touching event, the first day of school. A mother, especially, feels the poignant tug of separation as her sturdy child waves uncertainly and joins other anxious first graders in the biggest adventure of his life. For the parents of twins, the feelings of loss are not only doubled, they are mixed with uncertainty over the wisdom of the instructional policies of the school.

Will their little ones be separated in class, or will they be allowed to learn together? Yet, there they go, two children who may look alike and think alike, curious about the idea of school, unaware of the conflict they will face over the shaping of their minds.

There is misunderstanding, argument, conflict, and ambivalence over the separation of twins in their crucial early years. Spokesman for the National Organization of Mothers of Twins Clubs, Inc., mainly favor school policies that keep twins together in the class room, yet there are differences of opinions among these experts. On the other hand, authors who have made a speciality of studying twins in school insist that separation is usually best. In most school districts in the United States, the decision to separate twins, or not to, is arbitrary, depending on the whims of the classroom assignment process, unless parents express actual preference. And yet, the whole issue may be crucial to the twins.

I'll never forget being kept back in the fourth grade while my twin sister,Fay Louise, moved ahead. I'm sure it was the final proof I needed as a frail, indecisive child to convince me that I was inferior. For years, I believed I wasn't as smart as my sister. I refused to give myself any credit for having been ill and kept back for that reason. I was "dumb" and I played that record over and over, a thousand times.

Because the issue of separation is so important to the parents of twins and to the process of learning for the children involved, in 1984 I wrote to the State Superintendent of Schools for each of the 50 States with the purpose of discovering if there was a fundamental shared policy of placement of twins in classrooms.

Overwhelmingly, the responses indicated that no clear rules have been laid down. There are no specific guidelines for twins. This was still true when I talked with M. Eugene Wallace, Jr., in February of 1991. He is associated with the Office of Administrative Services of the Georgia Department of Education. Wallace conducted a "very unscientific" survey of nine out of Georgia's 187 school systems. He asked the questions I had posed in my letter:

1. Is special care taken to separate or keep twins together in the lower grades?
Four said their practice is to separate twins.

63

One said they place students alphabetically, therefore, twins would stay together unless parents request otherwise. One said they place students by ability, therefore, twins may or may not stay together. Usually they do unless parents request otherwise.

2.Do parents seek guidance in the placement of their twins? All nine systems said that some do and some don't.

3.Do you have a psychologist trained in this area? None of the people to whom I talked were aware of specific training in the placement of twins but all systems had access to the services of a psychologist if needed.

Most of the replies to my questions simply stated that there was no written policy concerning placement of twins or special care for them in the lower grades. Each child is placed in a classroom according to his or her abilities.

Some school superintendents said that it was a matter of individual teacher's opinion, in many cases, as to whether or not twins were separated in classrooms.

It's obvious from the results of my informal survey that, largely, parents make the choice for their children. And if they have a preference, they must make it clear to the teacher. This being so, it is vital for parents to understand the emotional repercussions that may develop in their twins as a result of a decision to separate or to keep them together. Often parents wrongly assume teachers understand the special qualities and importance of the twin relationship and about the normal range of disparities in the development between twins. Failure to recognize the normal "lags" between the children can result in school progress decisions that can adversely affect both twins for the rest of their lives.

I remember a woman who wrote to me still bitter in her middle years over the lack of sensitivity of her parents to her need to be her own person.

"I wanted to be separated from my twin in school, " she said. "But they treated us like babies all our lives. They treated us as a pair, rather than two individuals who looked alike. It was unfair to both of us, and it deprived us of the encouragement to strike out on our own. I resent that."

Parents are often bewildered about any advice that seems to favor one child over the other. Teachers recommendations to promote one twin in school in advance of the other are difficult to accept. A distraught mother said to me, "I just returned from a parents/teacher conference and I don't know what to do. The teacher recommended that my son repeat the first grade next year while his brother goes on to second grade. I know he is less mature than Brad and still has a hard time sitting for long periods, but this doesn't seem like the right thing to do."

It is difficult for parents to always make the correct decision. We will explore in this chapter the do's and don'ts of separation, the unresolved anger of twins toward their parents for not "protecting" the twinship, the benefits of placing twins apart, the problems of competition and comparison that arise between twins in the same class, and the necessity for adults to often rely on their intuition as the best judge of the readiness of their twins to accept individual placement in school.

Typical of many stories I've heard from twins who felt that separation was injurious to at least one half of the twinship was the narrative of L.M. who grew up in Portland, Oregon. She wrote:

"My brother and I were (separated) at the kindergarten level in school only to be reunited later in junior high. At this time I know it was intensely important to my parents that we both do well. It seems to me now that this (re-uniting) was sort of setting us up to be competitive. I can remember clearly report card day when Dick might have gotten better grades and then be deemed to be the more aggressive one.

"This competitive situation had interesting results. I started to be interested in learning and instead of breezing by I started to do well. On the other hand, Dick started hanging out with a rebellious group of people and ended up dropping out of school. I can remember feeling a horrid sense of relief and a consequent sense of guilt that I was responsible for screwing up Dick's future. Only now, six years later, is Dick getting back his self confidence when it comes to school. Given two insecure kids, it seems inevitable that this kind of circumstance is not productive."

Probably no issue involving twins has more of a divisive nature then the whole matter of separation in school. The ambivalence of educators throughout the U.S. to the problem of separation of twins was evident in the negative responses I received to my letter asking for information on policies on the subject.

Frankly, there is not enough information on the subject to form a reliable reference file by which parents may be guided. The one refrain which does seem to be dominant among teachers is that separation, especially for identical twins, is important to help each child express his individuality at an early age. But this idea is opinion, not a result of hard research evidence based on interviews with twins and parents of twins.

The fact is twins face a double separation when they enter school if they are placed apart. One is the separation from their home, the other is separation from one another. The emotional upheaval may be so disturbing that the twins may act out disruptive behavior for their teachers. Two children who had been model youngsters suddenly are threatened with the disintegration of a unique relationship and they may respond with anger and resentment.

No one denies the value of individuality and the desirability of encouraging twins to assert independence. The tricks seems to lie in timing. I have talked with hundreds of twins, identicals and fraternals, and the majority of them agree that separation is crucial to the achievement of independence. All of the twins, I think, were aware of the danger of over-reliance upon one another. They do not resent it as much as they are concerned that if one twin is deprived of the other by death or marriage or job re-location, the deserted twin would be the wounded half of what had been a perfect pair.

Barry Baatz of South Orange, New Jersey said that sharing Kindergarten prepares twins for separation when they are old enough for the first grade.

"At least we had one year together, " Barry said, "to see how we would act with other students. We knew that we could survive alone because we could see each other at break times. It was also a good chance to make new friends."

An identical twin from Charleston, Maine, Ann Race, voted for separation as necessary to building individuality. She said: "My sister and I were together until the eighth grade. I think that the separation then was slightly traumatic, at least for me. I worried about what my twin was doing and there was jealousy and things like that. I think I may have adjusted better had we been separated right from the start. It takes away from your development to have every one making an issue of the two of you when you're in the same classroom."

If making the primary decision of separating twins is confusing and often guilt-ridden for parents, imagine those who are faced with keeping one twin back, while the other goes into the next higher grade. Such was the dilemma of Joyce Piner, a mother of twin boys who has been a teacher herself for many years. She wrote the following account, printed here with permission from NOTMC's Nortebook.

"Six years ago I made one of the toughest decisions of my

67

life. My husband and I decided, after much careful thought and many consultations with our twins' Kindergarten teacher to retain Twin B in Kindergarten. He qualified to be promoted, but we felt because of his immaturity he would not be ready for first grade. This is always a tough decision. But it was even tougher because it involved twins.

"I had visited the teacher before school started and told her I wanted her to observe my boys closely to determine readiness for first grade; I did not think either one would be ready. They had a lot stacked against them: they were boys, they had July birthdays, they were six weeks premature, and they were twins. Much of my teaching career has been spent teaching remedial reading on the junior high level; 80 percent of my students had been boys. I always believed that this was so because they had been expected to learn to read too soon. Research has shown that six-year old girls are usually more mature than six-year old boys. I did not want my boys to develop reading problems.

"Needless to say, the teacher was taken aback; she was accustomed to having to persuade parents to allow her to retain their children. In the fall, she thought they would be ready. By winter she wasn't sure. In the spring, she asked me what I thought about sending one on to first grade and keeping the other in Kindergarten. I knew she thought Twin B should be retained. This idea never crossed my mind, but then I thought, 'If I keep them together, which one do I sacrifice? Do I send Twin B to first grade with Twin A and let him fall behind, or do I keep Twin A back with Twin B and let him get bored?'

"The obvious answer was what I did. It was not an easy decision but it was the right decision at the time. The teacher said that by Spring when she asked Twin B a question, he would say, 'check with my brother.' He had become completely dependent on his twin. We can not separate them on the same grade level because the school here on the beach is small and there was only one section of first grade at that time; however, that was not the reason for retaining him.

"Twin B went through some difficult times with his peers, explaining how he 'flunked Kindergarten'; however, he has developed into his own person with his own set of friends and his own interests. He became a leader in his class instead of the follower that he would have been.

"There is a happy ending to this story---Twin B has been in the 99th percentile on all standardized tests from first grade on and last year he was identified as academically gifted by the guidelines used in our state. When this happened, I patted myself on the back for my 'great decision' and then Twin A was identified as academically gifted last summer, and caused me to begin second-guessing my decision. Did the extra year of maturity allow Twin B to develop to his potential,or would he have done so eventually any way? I guess any decision I might have made six years ago would have caused me to stop and wonder many times if it were the right one.

"If I had the chance to do this over again, I probably would wait and enter both twins in Kindergarten at age six; this would allow both of them time to mature, to grow physically and to have an edge in leadership. Hindsight is always 20/20.

"Twin B has always wanted to be a veterinarian. I have to feel that the extra year we gave him to mature may help him to achieve that goal.

"Sometimes he asks me if there is any way that we could catch him up and graduate with Twin A, and I know that it could be done. If/when he is ready, we will make another 'great decision'. (Twin A has offered to work a year and wait for him to go away to college at the same time.)"

Retention of one of a boy/girl twin pair is, perhaps, even more troublesome to decide since girls are known to mature faster than boys. The "gap" is especially apparent in those areas required for school performance. They include virtues such as attention span (being able to sit still), social maturity (cooperation with adults and school mates), language development and general adaptation to studies.

Most teachers who have had experience with children have already become aware of disparity in the maturation processes of boys and girls. The gap is wider in the primary grades and begins to balance out by the fourth grade. The gap appears again at puberty and closes as the emerging adults finish high school. This gap has special consequences for twins of different sexes. And it is unfortunate that teachers often suggest retention as a way to cope with developmental differences.

Hard on any child, retention can have extreme negative effects on the relationship between twins. The problems of loss of self esteem, and friends and repeating a year in a learning environment that is immature in relation to the child's age, produce feelings of resentment and inferiority that may never completely go away.

I felt a sense of failure when I was asked to repeat the fourth grade while my sister was promoted to the fifth grade. My retention was a result of my illness the previous year. I had missd a lot of classes. Already sensitive about comparisons people made between my sister and I, the loss of equal status in school was a blow to my pride.

Instead of being gradually resolved and forgotten, negative feelings about retention can become permanent. Once a twin has been kept back a year, he or she will most probably never catch up to the other twin later on by skipping a grade. There will be a discrepancy in class standing and perceived achievement for at least 12 years of school, and longer if the pair goes on the college. Nothing can ever change the fact that twins will always be twins: same age, same birthday. No amount of rationalizing and support can completely eliminate the natural conclusion of the one kept back that he or she is the "dumb one".

Many people tend to perceive twins as opposites side of a mirror---reverse images in a social looking glass---good and bad, clever and dull, pretty and homely. When, by accident or illness, one is a class ahead of the other, it is natural for many people to think or even to ask out loud, "What's the matter with your twin?"

The twins' relationship may deteriorate; jealousy, envy and other unpleasant strains may develop between the pair as they enter the teen years and they become acutely sensitive to peer relations and peer appraisals. Boys in the male/female twin relationship, are often "on the defensive", maturing more slowly physically and in related behaviors such as party/going and dating. If a boy has been kept back a grade in elementary school, feelings of inferiority and resentment of his sister can resurface later as harsh criticism of his twin.

The twin who progresses at the normal pace has a burden to carry also. She must cope with feelings of guilt, embarrassment and resentment at the "slow" twin and, often, a sense that she has "betrayed" the twinship.

At the grim end of such an unbalanced relationship, there is a strong possibility that a feeling can develop that the twinship must be sacrificed in order for each twin to be his or her own person. That is the ultimate message of school retention if the event degenerates to the point of despair between the twins and desspair and unresolved anger at the parents for not protecting the twinship.

A former Eugene, Oregon teacher, Jacque Brown, has little patience for school authorities who dogmatically insist on separation of twins because the act fulfills a philosophical requirement recommended by psychologists. She insists that fostering individuality at the expense of the children's basic welfare is cruel and wrong:

"Since I was an elementary teacher for 15 years I feel my opinions have more weight than the average. I strongly feel that adults must take their clues from the twins. If they wish to be together, why not? We don't try to make a left handed person right handed. Being a twin is very special, also very natural. We are not freaks. Most educators get overexcited about the prospect of having twins in school. Many parents read too many philosophy -type books written by people who are not twins and therefore do not have a complete understanding of twins. All the teachers and administrators that I worked with knew very little about twins. They were not open to even discussing keeping twins together.

"Some one, sometime said, " Jacque reported, "that twins should not be together, and educators seem to believe this without any intelligent questioning or reasoning. I strongly believe that with practical observation, a moderately intelligent adult can determine the extent of 'togetherness' twins need. In the fifteen years I taught grades one to six, I encountered many sets of twins. Most were well adjusted. Only two sets had severe problems. These two sets were separated when they wanted to be together. One set (girls, fifth grade) both ended up in the hospital and almost died because they wouldn't eat.

"Their doctor even had the parents separate them from their home. One of the twins was sent to live with grandparents. When counseling, drugs, etc., wouldn't work to adjust the children to separation, the parents finally said, 'enough' and let them be together as much as they wanted. Their health returned and have since graduated from college."

Confusing and contradictory as the opinions are on the merits of separating twins or keeping them together, the fact remains that overall experience seems to indicate that it is best for most twins to be placed apart at some point in their school history. And most of the twins I've interviewed agree. They point out several advantages to "intelligent separation", including the major ones that being apart decreases twin dependency, accelerates independent academic and social growth and reduces comparison and competition between twins. Important to twins is the "elbow room" apartness allows a pair. They each suddenly have space of their own to grow, to do things at an individual pace, not to have to think in the familiar groove of dualism.

Two comments from twins support the idea of separation as the freedom to learn, explore and create ideas and experiences as an unfettered person. A Bothell, Washington woman said, "I never had anything to myself. I shared everything. I hated it. I used to wish I had my own birthday, because birthdays are so special when you're young."

An identical twin in her mid-fifties wrote that she had "developed a social dependency through the teen years. When my twin and I were separated at age 17 to go to college, the joy of being a person, I mean an individual, was overwhelming. But it took years to develop a self image. Conversely, separation was painful."

A year in Sweden as an exchange student so opened the eyes of one twin that he said, "I guess I had the feeling of not being a twin for a year, and I loved it."

There are ways to soften separation of twins, as Sheila and Michael Siegal, social worker, doctor, and parents of twins, point out: "If twins are anxious about separation, having them carry a

73

picture of their twin sibling and allowing occasional visits to each other's classroom may be helpful. Parents and schools must be flexible, however, and if twins have significant separation problems, placement together for a time may be advisable. If twins are in one classroom, placing them in separate work groups will lessen competition and encourage independence."

Parents should also understand that separation of twins is not an unnatural act, for as Kay Cassill said in her book, *Twins : Nature's Amazing Mystery,* "In common with other infants, twins are not as slow as has been supposed in gaining a well-defined sense of who they are."

Her statement is reinforced by research in the past four years that has established the fact that the human brain is programmed before birth---maybe even at the level of the human cell---to perceive the uniqueness of the ego. The recognition of self, as distinct from anybody else, as distinct from a twin, is part of the cognitive and intuitive equipment a human brings into the world. If in the childhood of twins, the temporary submersion of the individual self in a dual entity provides a psychic protection for the children, then normally this gives way as each twin builds an edifice of "self" around his incipient ego.

This is a fancy way of saying each child learns he is a separate human with ideas and desires of his own. Loyalty, companionship and close identification may keep each child in sequence with his twin, but eventually the self emerges as distinctly individual in each twin.

Teachers fill critical roles in helping twins gain a sense of individual self and the human quality of respect for "me". When they are arrogant or less than sensitive to the unique relationship of twins, they can do harm thay may last for years. Susan Pellicano, 30, a fraternal twin wrote to me describing an incident in the fourth grade that affected her perception of her intelligence.

"The memory is vivid of my teacher when she publicly announced to the class that my sister had scored higher in a test. I went home crying. Later, my parents talked to the teacher and I'll never forget her comment: 'Your daughters both have above average intelligence, which is unusual for twins.' I think after that I always felt handicapped. I was doomed to be average and 'lucky' if I earned 'As' and 'Bs' in my classes.

Barry Baatz, who reported earlier on Kindergarten experiences remembered his experience in the seventh grade as one which was humiliating. "We were sitting next to each other (my twin and I) and she (the teacher) came by and embarrassed us in front of the whole class. She said, 'Are you two married to each other?' I guess she didn't realize that we sat next to each other because we just wanted to sit next to each other."

As custodians of the process of emergence, of guiding their twins through the minefield of childhood dos and don'ts, parents need to be aware of their own affect on the formation of their children's intelligence.

It was made clear in the preceding chapter that there is absolutely no physiological difference in the intelligence of twins and single-born children, but parents of twins must be aware of the effect of lack of proper attention to their twins during the formative years. Often, overworked parents of twins simply don't have the time to give the children the early verbal encouragement that has been identified as a key stimulus for developing the groping mind. Also, since twins have each other, their sense of self sufficiency often distracts the parents from the task of preparing them to think individually. The youngsters appear not to need as much attention as single-born children. Any slowness on the part of twins in early childhood usually disappears by the time the twosome enters school.

The problem of lack of attention was addressed in a Harvard University study with orphan babies. Doctors Burton White and Jerome Kagan have demonstrated that lack of stimulating experiences in a busy home has a dulling effect on infants. The men discovered that dramatic differences in infant mental and personality development are attained through training in the crib.

Kagan said, "The baby is a novelty-digesting machine that devours change. Pushing him to new experiences keeps him moving."

From this study and others, psychologists studying twins have concluded that the contributions of parents to the mental development of their twins cannot be overestimated. The richness of their communication and understanding will have a profound effect on the brightness, verbal facility, motivation and general happiness of the children.

Many other factors influence the ability of twins to do well in school. These involve speech and gross motor skills, social maturity and a feeling of confidence imparted to them by their parents. According to Jesse R. Groothius, M.D., "Research suggests that twins may be more prone to many problems in each of these areas. Being aware of this fact could help parents and school personnel anticipate difficulties and initiate appropriate testing and support as problems surface. Neither parents nor school personnel should fall into the trap of expecting the twins to develop at an equal academic and social pace, nor should they dismiss problems lightly as 'single problems'".

"Most twins," says Dr. Groothius, "progress at different academic and social rates. If one twin is having problems in these areas, involvement in special hobbies or sports were she/he can excel independently will help the child compensate. Dr. Barton Schmitt feels that this added dimension will promote a sense of self worth and lessen the feeling of competitiveness and failure. It may also help to lessen the potential for school avoidance, cheating and social isolation."

Twins or singletons, all children, try to skip the roll call at one time or another during the grammar school years. The stomach ache or the headache are examples of excuses to avoid going to school. I believe a healthy child should not be allowed to stay at home just because his twin is really ill. Sympathy pains may develop into true school avoidance. If symptoms persist, parents should identify specific problems at school, such as favoritism, school studies, or teasing from other children, and work at school with teachers to resolve the problem.

Temperamental similarities and differences are another way in which twins are compared. Such comparisons may serve a purpose when they result in better understanding of twins as individuals. Twins do share a lot of experiences and they learn a lot about emotional responses from each other. But comparisons cease being useful when they cause parents or any one else to expect that one child should act like another.

Elvin Mills, 47-year-old, living in Junction City, Oregon, told me that "My twin always did better in his studies than I. Our report cards were always compared and I often wondered after we were out of school if I just quit trying because he was better at book studying."

Sheila, living in Houston, Texas, wrote, "I hated always having a brother in the same grade. Even though we never shared classes we did share the same teachers. I always felt I was being compared and checked up on. I was always expected to excel in the areas in which he had excelled."

Because twins are similar or often identical in appearance and actions, other people have unreasonable expectations that they should be the same in manner and behavior which only further encourages parental expectations for children to be the same. Each twin has a right to be himself and to develop at his own rate.

Angela Cross, a fraternal twin, living in Cheney, Kansas, reflected on her feelings about her twin in school. "I feel my twin should never have been scolded for getting a half a grade lower than me in subjects. I feel we were compared gradewise too much."

Daniel Whittaker, an identical twin, had some strong feelings about the expectations of adults regarding twins: "The negative about our childhood was the comparing and the competing. Because of this there developed hard feelings between us sometimes. There were frustrating moments and it all stemmed from the comparing and the competition.

"What was positive was that finally after about 18 years, we realized that we were who we were and we started voicing our own identities as individuals. We are now best friends and we have found some peace between ourselves."

To some degree, the twins themselves can encourage or discourage comparison. If they continue to capitalize on their sameness by dressing alike and always appearing together, they are encouraging the deadly game of comparison. While some twins don't mind comparison, most hate it.. A minority feel that comparison and competition spur them to greater achievement. Without question the majority feel comparison brings on resentment or lessens striving for accomplishment.

An identical twin woman living in Canada said to me at a twins conference, "I often felt resentment and anger at the comparisons, particular of the underlying feeling that we had to be the same."

Doctor Harriet H. Barrish of Kansas City, Missouri makes the observation that comparisons between children, or of the same child at different times definitely shapes our expectations of a particular child's behavior. If expectations become goals for training they can be helpful, but if they become demands that each of a pair of twins behaves a certain way all of the time, or be influenced to do something which he is not capable of doing, parent and child are being set up for frustration and anger.

Expectations put pressure on the child to perform in a certain way and the youngster may not be ready or willing. Parents should also recognize that twins who share a lot of experiences sometimes develop reciprocal or complimentary traits. One twin is active, the other passive. One is aggressive, the other is shy. One seeks adult approval, the other is more independent.

The success of social relationships of twins in school will depend to a great extent on the environment that children have at home. If the twins have confidence in the love and patience of their parents, many of the surprises they spring on their mother and father will be taken in stride as part of the development of the pair who share feelings, experiences, and even thoughts far more intimately than single-born children.

It seems quite obvious that sharing on all the levels that twins do, from looking and dressing alike, to thinking, acting, and playing alike, creates a remarkable interdependent relationship between them. School challenges this relationship. It demands of twins that they fit into a social dynamic composed of ordinary individuals who have a common goal. Twin children who enter into this fabric of learning are examined and marked for their curiosity. Twins stick out; they are exceptions to the rule of common identification and they are treated as strangers until gradually socialization rubs off their difference and fits them into the pattern of school life.

Doctor Lawrence J. Schweinhart, co-director of the Center for the Study of Public Polices for Young Children at The High Scope Educational Research Foundation of Ypsilanti, Michigan, adroitly summarizes for parents the challenge of guiding their twins with confidence, understanding and love:

"While being a twin presents special challenges in developing a sense of self identity, it also offers special opportunities. A twin provides his co-twin with a reflection of who he is and who he can be. Your twin can teach you your own strengths and weaknesses. Parents of twins share in these challenges and opportunities as the guides of their children down similar yet individual paths of development. They can enjoy and share in their children's initial similarities and emerging differences.

"By trying to encourage a particular ability to be equally developed in each of their children, parents are often using a sort of tunnel vision which results in overlooking many other skills and abilities which are present in each child."

CHAPTER VI

Sisters Remember: *The Struggle For Identity*

Author Karen Casey in her book, *The Love Book*, poignantly characterized the struggle for identity that is part of growing up for all children. It is especially fitting for twins:

"As children we clung to and modeled ourselves after friends and siblings and sometimes parents. We imitated with ease how a friend walked and gestured. At times we identified too closely and lost the self that ached to be known"

Adolescent years are crucial ones for any youngster. The whole question of "Who am I" becomes magnified in the eyes of a teenager. These are the years of strong hormone development, boiling new desires, agonizing self definition and a yearning for self expression through sexuality and the establishment of the attitudes of adulthood.

If they are exciting, bewildering and and difficult years for singletons, imagine the adjustments that twins have to make, especially identical twins. Changes that single children take all too easily for granted are ones twins often confront as obstacles as they try to strike a balance between the desirable aspects of being twins and the choices that make for individuality.

If the relationship between the twins is a healthy balance of shared ideas and recognition of the benefits of developing their separate individuality, then the parents can feel blessed. If, on the other hand, one of the twins emerges as dominant, exercising, "parent-like" influence over the other, then the relationship that results can produce serious emotional repercussions in the twins' future.

I am fortunate to have played the role of confidant to two remarkable identical twin women who were willing to share with me the consequences of the ambivalent relationship that started between them when they were small. By the time the parents recognized what was happening a pattern of behavior between the two had been set that would irrevocably affect their future decisions about their educations, careers, dating, marriage, childbearing and their ability to give love and return it.

I met Trudy Fast and her identical twin, Judy McCormick in Secaucus New Jersey in 1988 while I was attending the International Twins Convention. At that time they responded to my Twin Survey Questionaire. The correspondence and telephone calls that resulted from the contact created a bond of mutual interest between them and myself. I told them that eventually I would like to share their experiences in a book I planned to write. As it turned out, their special story emerged. It is told by Trudy Fast.

When Judy and I grew up it didn't take long for me to know that I could control my sister. Control meant manipulation. If she was playing with a doll that I wanted to play with I merely took it from her. No questions were asked. Often, Judy would come up to me and ask, "May I go to the library after school ?" and I would reply, "Just make sure you're home for dinner."

I became the mother figure to her and she would do anything to please me. Many times I placed Judy in a no- win situation. If she received and A on a report from school, I called her teacher's pet or a brown nose. If her grade was bad, I'd call her stupid, or worse. I would not speak to her especially if she excelled at something. I'm not proud of my actions then, I'm just stating a fact.

A child as young an impressionable as I was should never have had so much power over another person's life. We were both straight A students until the sixth grade. It was then my father finally realized how much I intimidated Judy and insisted that we be separated. I can still hear Judy screaming and holding on to me for dear life when we were told to report to different classes. I was excited and thought that it was really neat that I wouldn't have to have my twin hanging around my neck and vying for my attention.

It was also during this period that I stopped dressing like Judy. She was devastated. But there was a deep need in me to be different, to be an individual. I just wanted to be Trudy I was tired of people getting us confused, mixed up with one another, and I was tired of making all of Judy's decisions for her.

Later, in adult life, when Judy started having anxiety attacks I did a lot of reading and became convinced that her anxiety was the result of our having been separated in school and the fact that I no longer dressed like her. She felt rejected, and I, in my immaturity, encouraged it. Judy began to become a perfectionist. Although her grades slipped, she cried all the way to school because she was afraid she was going to be late. She bit her fingernails until they bled.

She did everything in her power to please everyone.

EVERYONE. And though I manipulated her, I was also protective. I remember one night we went to a dance and Judy accidentally bumped into a girl who shoved her. I screamed at the girl, "Knock it off. Don't you ever touch my sister again." She screamed back, and Judy moaned as the girl and I yelled at one another, "It's my fault. I'm sorry, I'm sorry." I was being tough and Judy was apologizing. Of course, in the end, everyone thought Judy was sweet and Trudy was the bitch.

I used to get sick when I saw others take advantage of Judy or use her. I guess it was o.k. for me to do it, but I couldn't see that then. Judy discovered a high school sweetheart, transferred her dependency to him, and I felt threatened by her new relationship. I tried to jeopardize it by not giving her phone messages to her; I told her unkind things about him. Despite my disparaging remarks, she became dependent on him, healthier mentally, and enlivened by her new outlook, she sought other girls to be with who were as domineering as I had been. Not surprising, I looked for new friends, male and female, weaker than myself. Obviously, each of us was pursuing the same role with others we had practiced between ourselves.

When Judy became homecoming queen in our senior year, she was astonished that she had been selected instead of me. It was painful for her to be pleased that she had been chosen. She hated to be envied for any personal success. It wasn't until we both went away to separate colleges that we experienced temporary role reversal. I went to Miami University, but missed Judy so much that I came home. I was astonished and hurt when a week later she left for Ohio University. I was certain she would stay home with me. But she literally ran away from home. Her high school boy friend joined the Army and Judy proved to be strong enough to go to college and survive without him or me.

Typically, the man I choose as the partner in my first marriage was weak. Is it surprising, given my need to dominate and Judy's to follow, that I talked her into a double wedding ? She married her high school sweetheart after a two-year separation from him while he was in the Army. He was a man upon whom she could rely to tell her what to do. It was only a year later that she fled the marriage, announcing she was getting a divorce. I said I'd get one too, completing again the circle we kept repeating of rejecting the influence of the people we'd chosen to be substitutes for her submissiveness and my need to dominate.

For the next five years, we demonstrated a dozen times our preferences for re-enacting these models of emotional instability. I would be attracted to someone who needed me, and then get burned out taking care of him. Judy would get involved with someone who would dominate her and get upset because he did what she expected him to do. Finally, at age 30, Judy joined the Army. I felt relieved but resentful. The Army was taking my place. I had two children who were draining me as a single parent, but at the same time I was jealous of Judy. She was told what to wear, where to work, what to eat. I believe her period in the military was the time when Judy was the healthiest mentally. The Army became her twin sister. No one ever adjusted to Army life the way Judy did.

I tried to block Judy from my mind. I refused to write to her. Then I fell in love with a practicing alcoholic. Guess what ? He needed me. He took Judy's place, but accused me when he was drinking of controlling him, "Just like you do your twin."

I was still resentful of Judy when my mother, my older sister and I visited her after she'd been in Germany for two years. I just couldn't believe she was happy and loved Army life. How dare she! Well, it took about one hour alone with her for me convince her that *he wasn't as happy as she said she was and couldn't possibly manage her life without me. I worked fast. It was all down hill from then on. When we met her the first day in Germany she was considering making the Army a lifetime career. When we left, she was crying, home sick and desperate for me to tell her what to do with her life. I had won. I was in control again. Judy still had about six months to go in the Army but they proved to be the longest six months of her life. She wrote to me two or three times a week, home sick, depressed, needing me. I told her to come home and I would take care of her.*

It is fascinating how self deceptive we can be. How we inch toward our own disaster. Judy moved to Florida from Germany, then to Georgia, then to Columbus, Ohio, then to Carey, Ohio, one hour from Toledo and me. Each new location was a step closer to our reunion and the reestablishment of the old pattern of tyranny and submission. Judy remarried and my husband went into alcohol recovery treatment, with me learning beside him. A new, fine relationship emerged between us. But Judy was in trouble. The man she had married was like quicksand, refusing to give her support equal to the domineering influence I had exercised over her.

Overwrought, Judy collapsed, got tranquilizers from a physician and quit her job because her panic attacks were too much for her to handle. Finally, after several months, I convinced Judy to go into an anxiety clinic. After 15 weeks of therapy she came out feeling on top of the world. I was included in her therapy, helping her to recover by encouraging her independence. That was my job. Ironically, the person who had contributed the most to her submissiveness, I, was the principle force to help her find herself.

Now, we see each other once or twice a month. Both of us restrain from any more frequent contact. We know its the best thing for her and for me. Just as I had to work hard to repair my marriage to an alcoholic, I have to work hard at repairing my life with my twin. It's a painful road. No one can make me feel as good about myself as Judy can and no one can ever make feel as pained. It took therapy for both of us to get our lives together and I continue to remind myself almost daily to "let go." I have made every major or minor decision for Judy for 40 years and it was hard for me to change, but by God, Judy's mental health was at stake. Just before the annual Twins Convention, Judy and I sat over a beer and Judy said, "Trudy I love you so much, but you consume me. I'm healthiest when I'm away from you."

If parents could anticipate the trouble an unbalanced relationship between their twins could bring to their adult lives, I'm sure they would be more careful about monitoring the early childhood years of their twins. Judy and I continue to be careful about falling back into the old pattern, and it's working out pretty well.

Is the relationship Trudy described a true reflection of how most identicals learn to adjust to one another and overcome the painful seesaw of dominance and submission? What is a normal relationship between twins?

Parental guidance is, above all, the most important factor in the shaping of the character and personality of twins. The degree of their cooperation, the affection they have for one another, the fluency of their interdependence, their emotional health and their ultimate success as adult humans, depend considerably on the manner in which their parents have encouraged the development of their individual self esteem.

But are Trudy and Judy typical of identical twin women? Yes and no. They represent one face of twinship, when one twin becomes overly dominant and suppresses the will of another. They felt that by sharing their experience it would alert parents of twins to be more aware of what can happen when one twin assumes a dominant role. As I talked with both Trudy and Judy in person I sensed the love they have for each other. Had they not loved each other they would not have searched to correct what it was in their relationship that caused their pain.

In most identical twin relationships there is a healthy exchange of give and take. Fraternal twins are more likely to be subject to dominance of one over the other because of the great differences between the two. Being no more alike than any other siblings they may be very different in temperment. They may be more "normal" than identicals.

If "normal" means well adjusted, able to enjoy life, give love and accept it without guilt, and take part as wholesome, contributing adults in society, then the men and women twins who answered questions in my survey are as typical as any sample of Americans. They come from all types of homes and jobs from Alaska to Maine, from Hawaii, Europe and Australia.

The comments they have made overwhelmingly substantiate the importance of parents as loving caretakers who value and gently encourage the development of individuality in their twins and who are fair and competent as arbiters of childhood disputes. Those who show favoritism and make unfair comparisons are setting the stage for bitter rivalry between twins that may drive them apart at some point in their lives, or create an unhealthy relationship in which one rules the roost over the other.

One twin wrote me of smoldering rancor that surfaced between her brother and her after 40 years:

"My brother used me as a mother substitute for many years. Therefore I gave him the advice he asked for, and he became dependent on me. One day, recently, at age 40, he woke up and started to make his own decisions. It's great for him and now he hates me. I don't care because I never wanted to be a mother to him and I never asked for the role. I just let it happen".

A California male twin, Steve said:

"My sister and I were allowed different privileges mostly due to the fact that my parents felt they could trust me more than they could her. We were always referred to as 'the twins'. It wasn't until my senior year in high school that I finally felt a good affection for her."

A twin who got tired of being known as "Tom's brother", struck the plaintive note that many twins echo when they remember their feelings of dependence on their twin:

"The most negative aspect of my being a twin was my dependency on my brother. He was my protector and I couldn't do without him, but in time this feeling drew us farther apart. I resented him because I couldn't function on my own. I think the turning point in my life came in my senior year in high school. I became strong enough to insist on my own sense of self. I just got tired of being known as Tom's brother."

A twin who characterized her sister as a "mother hen" told of her anguished years trying to establish her separate identity.

"My adolescent years were difficult because my twin was a real achiever and I felt I had to keep up. Yet, I had a different mind set, a different personality I needed to explore. Sure, it was great to always have a playmate and best friend. During the adolescent years, though, we were separated mentally, and that was the worst time for me. Sylvia and my parents were always on the 'good side', and I was this 'bad seed' pitted against them. Sylvia was the mother hen, always correcting me, putting me down, and I think this contributed to my identity problems later in my life---the lack of security and the need for constant praise. Even though I have sorted most of this out in therapy, the insecurity lingers."

If there is a singular message that emerges from the comments of these twins, it is that when each one of a pair feels good about himself, truly recognizes his special oneness as a human being apart from his twin relationship, then he has the foundation to feel safe as a partner in a twinship. My own research shows that this sought-after balance of compatibility and equality between twins, as reflected in my survey showed a frequency of about 15 to 25 percent. This was expressed by a 40-year old California female who wrote to me:

"Mom and Dad helped us discover our natural talents and nudged us to cultivate them. I was good at art. Peg was terrific at the piano. Our folks were wise enough to gently urge us to encourage the other person's gift and not try to compete with her in her area of expertise. It was a great idea. Each of us developed her own ability and in the process learned to respect one another. It was the basis of a life time of collaboration and cooperation. We have to thank our folks for the wisdom to set us on the right path."

There is a pattern that seems to repeat itself in the lives of some twins, that shows up when the pair has matured. The one who has been the follower, or slower, or less aggressive, suddenly declares independence. This usually happens when the twins have separated and have developed some independent experiences. The sudden "standing up" of the submissive twin many times results in a permanent rupture of the established relationship between the pair. If the love that binds the pair together is strong enough to absorb the shock of the rupture, the new relationship that emerges will survive, in many cases, much stronger than the former one that was unequal.

A remarkable demonstration of this development was the thoughtful letter written to me by a 40-year old twin, a journalist, who traced the relationship between herself an her sister. Kathy's poignant description not only touches the heart, but provides an important message for parents concerned that competition and rivalry between their twins will eventually create a rift that may be difficult to repair. Following are excerpts from Kathy's letter:

We were as close as any twins can be. We had our own private language, we shared the same class room until the sixth grade, and when we entered junior high school we dressed alike, as emotional support, until we had adjusted to the "new" situation. Whenever Karen was having a tough time with her school work or love life, I was always there to listen to her. I was her mom away from home. Life always seemed more settled for me and I didn't have as many emotional needs.

I don't think the competition between us will ever end. Yet, I don't think I ever consciously competed with my sister. During our growing -up years we would "step back" if one was better in a certain area. She cooked and I drew. Those were our talents. We never tried to develop each other's talents. It was as if we wanted each other to look good. Karen used to tell me she envied my spirituality, but I think it was her drinking and the deeds she did in those times, plus the guilt and her conscience that kept her from feeling spiritual. I guess she envied the involvement that my husband and I had in a Catholic bible-sharing group.

It is strange to have a mirror, though not always pleasant to look at her and see my faults reflected back. It is usually the traits you hate in yourself that color your attitude toward a child who has them or keep you from enjoying a friend. And it's those negative traits you see in yourself, and again in your twin, that smack you in the face. I'd say my competition is with myself, not with her.

A few years ago she had breast implants which I tried to talk her out of. It would make us look different and I wasn't ready for that. But she did it anyway and they're big, and now when I'm on the beach I feel like the "Before and After" for a bust development

*commercial. I feel like hanging a sign that says "Mine are real".
Anyway, competition is a funny thing between twins. I believe it's
part of the package, and I certainly feel we had very little.*

*Right now we're going through a new stage, or at least she
says she is. She wants me to know who she is. I feel like I know who
I am. She says I don't. So I listen to her. She is in a constantly
changing pattern. I think coming to terms with my Dad's
alcoholism, and she with hers, has caused both of us to questions
many aspects of our lives. I know I am an intense person, but
Karen is very intense. I tried to get her to lighten up and not take
the world so seriously. But she thinks I am trying to minimize her
place in life.*

*But I feel like protecting her from any more pain. She seems
to have had so many more crisis and more pain than I. We are type
A people, aggressive, introspective, talkative, and brutally honest
with everyone. Probably now, for the first time in my life, I can't be
sure she will agree with me on the larger issues. In the past, I could
absolutely depend on her or persuade her to my point of view. Her
behavior says to me that number two is coming of age, growing up
and becoming a "twin-dividual" (great word). The change in her is
surprising, but not disappointing. I look forward to a settling out
between us and a balancing in the future. We are both growing up
and that's good.*

Kathy's sister, Karen, responded to the letter Kathy wrote to
me in a manner that demonstrates the insight the submissive sister
has gained:

*In any relationship, if one person is the helper, the other the
helped, then the dominant one is sure to feel stronger, or smarter.
There will be competition, and feelings of insecurity between the
two. After our daughter was still-born, Kathy noticed I stopped
needing her. I started a support group in Houston and my needs*

were met by those with similar experiences. I let go of that group when I started to go to AA. My theory proved to be correct that I couldn't give strength to others when I had none to give. I have found the beginning of a new relationship with God through that program and a better understanding of how I leaned on my sister.

My move has removed me from the unhealthy past and from relationships I had with others in which I was the dominated one. I sense that I have always looked for affirmation from the outside through my appearance, my successes, and my friends, and of course my sister. My sense of who I am has become internalized and I'm beginning to have a healthy friendship with myself. Kathy has done her growing up. I feel comfortable now with my past and with the present and trust in God for the future.

There has been an increasing amount of discussion by parents of twins about the question of rebellion in the mature years of a twinship by the submissive partner in the pair. The discussion has revolved around how to prevent permanent breaks in twin relationships when the less aggressive twin insists on new rules of conduct in the twinship and acknowledgement of his reformed status.

Inevitably when this subject has come up, examples of twins who have bitterly parted company are given as justification to urge a policy in schools of separation of twins at an early age. The idea is that separation will encourage the development of independence in both twins sooner, forestalling ugly, heartbreaking "divorces" later on.

No statement could more clearly illustrate the buried hostility toward a twin and the relief of separation than the one from this middle-aged woman who told me:

"I have given a lot of thought to my twinship, often obsessed, horrified secretly, with the idea that I am an identical twin.

My sister's unattractive characteristics are more glaring than her attractive ones. I see all the unattractive ones reflected in me. I think my twinship arrested my personal development and growth. Now, at mid-life, I think I'm catching up. Perhaps it takes this long to become your own person anyway."

This woman's anger with her sister, her spoken desire to be disassociated with her, clearly demonstrates the heart of the debate heating up involving teachers and parents over separating twins in school. In Chapter V we discussed the lack of a uniform policy among our educators about dividing twins into separate school rooms. The educators argue that separation early, particular for identicals, is important to help each child to develop his own identity. Other educators insist that timing of separation must depend on how much independence is fostered in the home. Some teachers have asked parents to dress their twins differently, as a means of deemphasizing the uniqueness of twins---to make them fit into a class room environment with less attention.

Since there is no established policy regarding whether or not to separate twins, it seems reasonable to recommend that parents, teachers and twins cooperate to make the decision.

Since the years of puberty and beyond are the crucial ones in which most teenagers agonize over who they are and who they want to be in relationship to the larger society of which they now become more acutely aware, many twin researchers suggest that school separation during adolescence adds unneeded additional turmoil to the twins' general state of anxious quandary.

On the other hand, among the significant problems that come up when twins are kept together in classes or schools during these years of self examination are over- competitiveness, the "gang of two" syndrome, overdependency, and intellectual averaging to a common denominator.

As a result, some twins faced with the inner conflicts of adolescence, either retreat into their partnership farther, or insist on a dramatic split between themselves. Both alternatives can be harmful to each and the twin bond.

It would be unfair and incorrect to suggest that all twins have serious problems of adjusting to one another while they are children and when they are grown up. Many, especially identicals, are almost inseparable and glory in their duality. The Rainer twins, of Winston-Salem, North Carolina, have agreed to share their views on their twinship and they offer advice to parents and teachers on the question of twins developing individuality.

We are a 58-year-old set of very happy identical twins. We've been together all of our lives and still dress just alike all the time. It would feel strange and disturbing to us to look different by being dressed differently. For us to dress differently would be like a person having one kind of shoe on the left foot and another kind on the right foot. We do not even own any clothes, jewelry, or anything that is not exactly alike. We share everything---one condo, one car, one bank account, etc. and we do everything together, including our profession. We are concert piano-duettists---which means we even get to share the same piano at the same time. We like all the same things and do everything together. We can not imagine not doing things together and not sharing things. We can not even imagine not being twins.

We have two tiny toy poodles which we also share. One dog doesn't belong to one twin and the other to the other twin. Both poodles belong to both of us and we treat them just like we think all twins should be treated: exactly alike. They are fed at the same time and the same kind and amount of food, taken outside at the same time, hugged, kissed and loved at the same time (and also a lot).

Our advice to parents and teachers: Let the twins decide

how "twinsy" they want to be. Treat them exactly the same, give them everything just alike and dress them alike until they are old enough to decide what they want, just like any other child when he gets old enough to pick out his own clothes. Let the twins decide if they want to dress alike or be in the same room at school.

We think the biggest problem twins have is other people who don't understand them. We are very annoyed at people who say twins must develop their individuality. We don't think they should be individuals unless they decide they would rather be. It's not a thing anyone else should decide for them. Actually we think we are one person. And we've always been lucky enough to have a family and friends who know how we feel and who treat us accordingly. If we ever should come in contact with any person who favored one of us, neither of us would tolerate it, and we would immediately cease to have anything whatsoever to do with that person. It has never happened but we know we would not have it.

Being twins is fun. It's wonderful! It's everything good that twins say it is---always having a good friend, always having someone to talk to, to do things with, to share things with. Why should someone else take those things away from twins by separating them and by insisting that they become "individuals" (whatever they think "individuals" are)? Why should anyone decide they have the right to deprive twins of their many pleasures? We were lucky, first by being born twins and second by being born into a family who let us be what we are, and third by having friends who understand us. Yes, we are very fortunate and very happy.

It is quite obvious from the experience of twins related in this chapter that parents of twins are presented with a heavier burden of responsibility than they carry for their singleton children in the family. The January/February 1987 issue of Twins Magazine addressed this dilemma of parents in a remarkably clear and provocative fashion. Authors Patricia Edmister and Georgia Lewis advised parents to develop safe risks for their twins as a means of training them in self reliance and independent thinking:

"Teenagers need to develop self reliance, learn responsibility and acquire problem- solving ability. While some people seem to be born with such qualities, others can develop them through experience and encouragement. Parents play an important role in this process.

"As they did when the children were babies, wise parents allow their adolescent twins to explore their ever- expanding world within appropriate limits. Long before the time comes to leave home, teenagers should acquire survival skills. Unfortunately, only limited opportunities exist today, especially in suburbia, to learn these skills 'naturally'. Sheltered and isolated, today's teens seldom explore the wilderness, the working world, or any environment different from their own neighborhoods.

"'Many of our kids are so protected from danger that they become afraid, once wrote syndicated columnist Ellen Goodman, 'so sheltered that they are unable to cope with their first harsh encounter or reversal; so unable to assume responsibility that they end up feeling responsible only to their whims'.

"Parents, then, need to structure and encourage experiences that will support their children's emerging independence under positive conditions. Yet one of the most difficult tasks of parenthood is to balance protection with letting go."

As a twin myself, and a parent, I vote my support for these thoughts because such conditioning prepares twins for independence from one another. Independence does not, in any sense, mean desertion. It means, basically, the flowering of the valid kernel of individualism every human has the potential to make bloom. As I review the hundreds of answers to the questionaires I sent to twins all over the United States, I am always struck by one common theme that emerges: *I love my twin and I don't want to hurt him, but I need to find out who I am.*

A 25-year-old identical twin expressed frustration over her need to be recognized as an individual at the expense of her twin:

"A child learns at an unusually young age how to compete for the feelings that a single child would feel at the same young age---the feeling that there is an identity that is distinctive only to that one child. There is no need for the single child to prove to anyone that she is the one and only special person in her parents lives. There is a feeling, bordering on self preservation, that a twin feels naturally, from the time she starts to interact with people. It is a feeling that she must win the affections of family, friends, and anyone who matters in her life. This feeling is similar to the feeling that the prospective employee might feel during a job interview. Impress and charm. In some cases, at any cost. In the case of twins, it can result in carefully, oh-so-subtly, making your twin seem like less the person in comparison. Once again, this feeling is not intentional. It is a natural feeling that comes on so gradually that it is hardly noticed until it is an emotion that is difficult to control."

Parents can aid their twins in the discovery of their single selves, and strengthen the bond of twinship, if they will create challenges that test their twins' growth, build their self esteem and provide them with the confidence to step outside the protection of their twinship. This is the first big step to maturity.

Here are a few tips to parents for teenage guidance and character-building for their twins. They are reprinted with permission from *Twins Magazine*.

* Help your children build confidence by accepting challenges that carry a high probability of success. Support them as

they explore new activities, but don't force them to participate in those of your choice or to be involved in the same activities.

* Don't assume each of your twins will be involved in the same activities.

* Give sincere encouragement, not false praise. Convey an attitude of "You can do it!" Twins often perform this "cheerleader" role for each other.

* Don't emphasize success so much that your teens will be devastated by failure. Value the adventurousness, spirit, and courage it takes to try.

* Beware of boredom! It can lead to foolish risk-taking. Work with others in your community to provide healthy, safe activities.

* Without resorting to scare tactics or exaggerations, discuss drugs, alcohol, suicide, and pregnancy with your teens. Let them know you are available to help.

* Prepare your twins for new experiences, one step at a time. For example, travel a new route with them before they try it alone. Let them try it together before they do it separately.

* Encourage twins to face scary new experiences together, but don't overdo it. They can't always look out for each other, and it's important for each to try doing some risky things alone.

Twins Magazine also published an excellent guide to help adolescents reject dangerous challenges. With permission it is reprinted here. If all parents, those who have twins in the family, and those with singletons only, adopted these words to live by, there would be far less "juvenile delinquency" and a far greater number of kids who respect their mothers and fathers.

* Don't stop setting limits just because your children look grown up. With your children's help, modify your family rules to reflect their new maturity.

* Teach your twins to think about the consequences of their behavior. Much risk-taking is impulsive. Typical teens do not naturally consider what might be the results of a particular act.

* Plan ahead for emergencies by discussing "what if?" questions, such as: " What if you have a flat tire on the way home?" or "What if your friends are all smoking pot at the party---what will you do?"

* Be ready to bail them out if your twins encounter a situation they can't handle. For example, by agreement one girl called her father for a ride home when her date, who was drunk, insisted on driving. Father and daughter had discussed this possibility before the party.

* When the issue is a dangerous one, such as drug use, help your twins understand the difference between harmless and harmful "secrets". Some twins develop a patterns of "covering" for each other to keep information from their parents, and this kind of twin closeness can be devastating. Tell them that safety and health issues must be handled openly and taken seriously.

* Encourage your twins to support each other when peer pressure seems overwhelming. Discuss ways to " say no".

* Finally, think about your own life and what you're modeling for your children. If you smoke, despite the documented risks involved, you're setting an example of risk-taking that is both dangerous and foolish. Conversely, if you remain in unsatisfying work out of excessive fear of the unknown or of failure, perhaps you're not providing the example of confidence and energy you would like your children to emulate.

The intimacy between twins can be so sensitive that it influences the manner in which they choose relationships with other people. Many twins say they have been spoiled for others by the bond of understanding between them---reflecting the unity that has emerged from years of friendship and rivalry, competition and love. As one twin said, remembering the school years and the adolescent ones, "He is my most beloved friend and my bitterest rival, my confident and my betrayer, my sustainer and my dependent, and scariest of all, my equal." The twin who made that remark, Gregg Levoy, in a thoughtful article in Psychology Today was expressing what most twins feel about their twin, but may not have the eloquence to say it as well.

The effort between twins to reach accommodation in their adult years is prodigious. As Kay Cassill wrote in *Twins, Nature's Amazing Mystery,* "There are probably few adult twins who don't carry some psychological scars from the prejudices they have endured in their formative years."

As I think back on the wisdom offered to me by the twins who have been subjects in my research for this book, I realize that Gregg Levoy hit the bullseye when he wrote that the task of twinship is indeed for twins to learn separateness---the grace and exasperation of individuality. He described the process with marvelous understanding in his Psychology Today article:

"By degrees, though, we conspired to step away from each other's shadow, and this, I think, is the task of twinship": Whereas others begin life separate and must learn intimacy, Ross and I began life intimate and had to learn separateness.

Every time someone would recklessly ask 'Which half are you?' or 'If I pinch you, will he feel it?' it became clearer to us that if for no other reason than novelty or convenience, we were seen as one entity. But we were not! That's what our fighting proved. And if I could be The Older One or he The Cute One, if I could be The Smart One or he The Artistic One, if, even for a moment, I could be the winner and he the loser, then by God we were not one entity."

CHAPTER VII

Marriage: *Matching A Mate With A Twin*

A feature in a tabloid newspaper printed in May 1989 carried the story of identical twins who shared a wife and happily raised the children of their three-cornered union.

According to the report, twin brothers Art and Bart Stevers are Australian fire fighters who love to play golf, eat pizza and come home to the same pretty redhead named Judy. She is the mother and the twins are the fathers of four children by her.

The twins are satisfied living as one big happy family with their wife, four children and two collies. The mother of the boys, Georgine, said that her sons never had any trouble getting girls, but neither of them had ever met someone special enough to settle down with until Judy came along.

Art met her while he was working the midnight shift. She was a new dispatcher. Three weeks later, Art's new girl friend was transferred to the day shift and met Bart who reported to his mother a few days later that he had met the girl of his dreams---the dispatcher who used to work nights.

Georgine said she was not surprised by the double attraction of her twins. "My boys have always liked the same things," she said.

Far from considering the triangle a threat to their close relationship, Art and Bart decided to share their favorite girl, with her permission. Judy didn't mind and soon the trio moved into her spacious home near Brisbane, Australia.

"We share everything in this house, including love," said Judy, pointing out that a practical sleeping arrangement was mapped out in which Judy shared Art's bed three nights a week, then transferred to Bart's bed for three nights.

"I don't count who gets the extra day," Judy said "Neither do they because in the end it all evens out."

Besides sharing the love making, the twins also share the parental responsibilities of their four children.

"We raise them all together as both our children," said Bart, pointing out that there was no way the twins could know who fathered which child. " Since they are all the same genetically, it just doesn't matter," Art said.

Although the Stevers kids take a lot of ribbing at school, they profess to love the unusual life style.

"It's like having two dads," said twelve-year old Lionel.

Though unusual, Art and Bart's connubial sharing demonstrates in the extreme the "couple effect" twins develop between themselves. And it is this affinity of feelings, thoughts, likes and dislikes, even sexual attraction to marriage partners, that make the matrimonial unions of twins among the best and the worst.

In Chapter I, I pointed out that it is often difficult and emotionally crippling for twins to pull away from one another as a result of marriage. Few are the generous, open, unjealous relationships typical of Art, Bart and Judy. For the majority of twins, identical or fraternal, the marriage of either twin can represent a feeling of loss and a threat to the twin bond. Fear of loss is the reason that more than 45 percent of all female twins, fraternal and identical, never marry, and that 25 percent of all identical male twins remain single.

A woman I met at the International Twins Association annual meeting demonstrates the heart ache twins can have when imposed separation, because of a jealous spouse, cuts them off from their twin.

In her sixties, this woman attended a workshop devoted to adjusting to the "loss of a twin" because, although she lived less than 100 miles from her twin sister, she had been deprived of her twin's companionship by her husband who resented her having contact with her twin. He was unreasonably jealous of the closeness of the two. It seemed as though her sister was " dead" to her and her grief was as real as if her sister had actually died.

This case demonstrates the regrettable failure of some non-twins to understand the deep and lasting attachments that develop between a high percentage of twins, most especially identicals.

A set of male twins who live in New Jersey would like to get married, but have admitted to me that they are afraid of the distance wives might put between them, unless the wives were twins themselves. They are determined to hold out for such a double union, even if it means they may never find twin females who would consent to marriage.

Often non-twins feel left out, jealous of a relationship they believe to be strange, unnatural and exclusionary, more typical of the sensitive communications that pass between older married couples who have learned to think alike. Such attitudes may be one of the primary reasons for the high celibacy rate among male and female identical twins.

I remember my own feeling of uneasiness about marrying before my twin did. We are fraternals, not as close as identicals are thought to be, yet neither Louise nor I were prepared for the separation that my marriage portended.

Louise had always beat me at having the first date and always had more boy friends, as many as three courting her at once. Yet, here I was, the first to leave home. The night before the wedding, Louise came into the upstairs bedroom and sat down on the bed as I busily tucked this and that into my going-away bag. All at once she started crying, then sobbed. I was caught off guard. I was happy; she was supposed to be that way too.

I like to think I rushed to her side and comforted her. I'm not sure that I did. As I look back on it now, I think I probably tried to reassure her that I was not leaving her for good and that I thought she'd soon be taking the same steps as I. I was right. Six months later we switched dresses and she walked the same isle in the same church.

Why was she crying? At no time had I ever given a thought that she might feel a sense of loss at my leaving. But why shouldn't she ? It was a normal response to a normal situation. She was not prepared for me to leave. I was not prepared to see her cry.

Bonnie Golliher, a Meade, Kansas fraternal twin, cautions twins to communicate with their spouses or risk the failure of their marriages.

"Be patient with your spouse, for it may hard for him to understand the feelings of twins. Keep communicating and communicating, because if you don't there will be problems.

"I know, " she observed, "for somewhere along the way in our relationship we stopped communicating and were divorced after 13 years of marriage and three beautiful children. He really had problems with the twin in my life."

Reliable statistics on twins and marriage and divorce are hard to find. However, Drs. Janet Kizziar and Judy Hegdorn, identical twins, suggested in their book, *Gemini---The Psychology and Phenomena Of Twins*, that divorces among identical twins are slightly higher than the average for singletons because the husband and wife relationship can never quite measure up to the closeness that identical twins share. This observation seems to fit with the statistics I quoted earlier on the high rate of abstention from marriage by identicals, male and female.

Recognition of the rights of the marriage and the rights of the twinship existing as a condition of the marriage are important considerations, observed the husband of an identical twin:

"I respect the twin bond an awful lot. I recognize my wife's need to see her twin as frequently as possible and I understand there is a need and love there that goes beyond a husband/wife relationship.

"I feel that there is a camaraderie between the twins that, while it doesn't threaten me, I know I need to make allowances for. For example, what might be secret between a man and a wife is not necessarily secret between a man, a wife and a wife's twin. I think that my wife's twin knows me very well because, in a certain way I am shared with her. I think my wife and her twin use both their lives as twins to validate their lives individually."

If validation continues to be an important factor in the individual lives of twins, the decision to embrace a wider world through marriage can be a hard choice. As Alice Vollmer wrote, "If twins are too attuned to each other and the spouse feels left out, the marriage and the twinship can be hard to reconcile."

This was the case with Bruce, an identical twin who lost his brother in an accident when both of them were 13-years old. The loss sent Bruce searching for someone who could take the place of his missing brother.

Years later, Bruce married and tried to establish with his new wife the bond of affection and empathy he had shared with his brother.

"My wife never understood," he said, "why I was always trying to be close to her. She was born and raised in a family that kept everybody at arm's length. She did not understand that my attempts at closeness with her were derivative of the bond that linked my brother and I. I didn't know, having no other brothers or sisters, that there was any other way of relating to somebody other than with the closeness I had had with my twin."

Bruce's wife, feeling smothered, met another man, fell in love with him and divorced Bruce.

For a single-born person, marriage to a twin unquestionably takes a special kind of understanding. Some have learned this to their dismay. In Australia, the husbands of identical twin sisters who, according to the sisters, were taking them for granted, got the surprise of their lives when the adventurous women switched places and households for two months, returning to their respective homes at bedtime.

Neither husband got wise to the switch until one day the twin named Maureen served the wrong brand of beer to her sister's husband, George. The masquerade ended, the subsequent furor was calmed, the husbands swore they would be more attentive, and the wives returned to their respective homes.

Because marriage of twins to singletons may pose some difficult problems, I visited with dozens of twins to develop a questionaire that may be helpful to both twins considering marriage and to singletons who are planning matrimony with a twin. If the issues represented in this questionaire are seriously discussed before the knot is tied, at the very least the new couple will be prepared in advance for some adjustments that their marriage is going to require them to make.

1. The twin who marries often feels guilty for leaving his or her twin. The comments of an identical twin from Washington illustrates both the problem of guilt and its solution: "I was the first to marry. When I told my twin that I was engaged I was excited. When I saw her response I felt angry, then I felt guilty. Her negative response to my engagement caught me by surprise because we had always had boy friends and there was never a problem with that. I think the finality of marriage and the fact that I hadn't known my fiance very long made us both realize that things were going to change. However by the time of the wedding we were both very happy and realized that the love I have for my husband cannot affect the love I have for my sister. We will never lose each other to anyone; we are simply facing new stages in our lives."

2. The twins may, after one is married continue their close relationship at the expense of the relationship between the new couple.

The lament of a woman divorced from an identical twin clearly illustrated that the man or woman who marries into a tight bond may often not feel secure about his or her standing in the marriage. One midwestern woman, married to an identical twin for over 30 years, ended the union with regret for lost hope and with sadness over her ex-husband's preference for companionship with his twin brother to the detriment of his relations with his own family.

"After many years I am still trying to understand the relationship between those two men. One of my children said one day that he hoped his uncle died first, then he might have some time with his own father. Of course, the kids feel guilty for feeling this way, but I certainly understand their emotions. After all, I played second fiddle as well.

3. A dependent twin left behind may continue to depend on his or her twin to help make decisions, thus competing with the spouse for time and attention.

This was verified by an identical twin in the Midwest who wrote: "If there has been any discernible effect of being a twin in a marriage it would be in the area of withholding communication from the spouse. There were times I would communicate information to my brother rather than to my wife. The appropriate line of communication should have been with my wife. I think this may have to do with the area of trust. I trust my brother implicitly whereas I have not done so with my wife. It also seems the love from my brother is unconditional, whereas the relationship with my wife has been more conditional."

4. If the spouse is of a jealous nature he or she may resent the continuing private relationship between the twins.

In this respect, a female twin observed: "I was married in 1970 and now I am recently divorced. My husband could never understand the closeness we (my brother and I) had. He was jealous of us and I couldn't make him understand."

5. If the twin spouse has previously been a dependent twin he or she may transfer that dependency to the marriage partner.

A twin in her middle years wrote: "I never gave myself the opportunity to develop my personality because I let my twin take charge. I broke our strong relationship by being the first twin to marry and now realize that I went from twin to husband tending to depend on them to take the initiative."

6. Here is a good example of a positive effect of twinship in a marriage as related by a twin: "I had a really wonderful marriage which was, in part, due to the skills of sharing and communication learned from my twin."

It would be remarkable and extremely helpful if twins and their spouses-to-be actually could discuss issues such as the ones I have listed. Realistically, it's probably too much to expect of twins to bring up such concerns which have deep roots in tender, carefully guarded emotions. But, oh, the pain and anguish that could be avoided if only they would. If the new spouse could only understand that often a twin is simply transferring the role he played in the twin bond to the marriage, then much heartbreak could be avoided.

Dr. Jane Greer, a twins consultant, speaking at the Sixth International Congress on Twin Studies in Rome, said that "By recognizing the importance of the twin relationship and dealing directly with the array of feelings that accompany it, a twin can bring the many positive, sharing aspects of the twinship into a marriage."

It is extremely important for twins to talk to their spouses-to-be about the feelings they have about their twinship. It is no less important, however, to have that same kind of conversation with their twin.

The need for the married twin and her new husband, or wife, as the case may be, to talk to one another with an open honesty and frankness that the new spouse may never have experienced, is paramount to the success of the marriage. At least the couple must begin the process of a different dialogue---because it is the surest path to head off jealousy. And taking care of the married twins' nervousness and fears are only half of the problem. Often there is jealousy, hurt or anger on the part of the twin who has been left behind. And sometimes there is just envy:

"It's like entering into a secret world that your twin can't experience," said an identical whose sister had married. "One of my most painful emotional experiences was when my twin married and left home before me. Both of us were anxious to experience sex, but not before marriage because of our upbringing. She was a virgin when she married. I envied her the feeling of love with her husband,

and although we could talk about anything I couldn't ask her what sex was really like. All of a sudden, she seemed more grown up than I because she had married."

Typically, twins compliment one another's behavior and often act as a unit in dealing with day to day matters. A Kansas woman told me, "My twin married and we both suffered a lot. I was really scared because for the first time I had to sleep alone, pay my own bills and be by myself. Never again will I be that close to anyone."

It's natural that twins grow up depending upon one another. Comfortable and convenient, it is a snug relationship for twins to fit in to. It's also easier to make decisions when two share the responsibility. Many twins have told me that the hardest part of first being separated was having to make decisions on their own because each of them had cooperated in a support dependency relationship. It's easier for two to walk into a new class room than for one. New situations are less threatening, new experiences less frightening, when there is a partner by your side.

"I never gave myself the opportunity to develop my personality because I let my twin take charge," said one twin. "I broke our strong relationship by being the first to marry and now realize that I went from twin to husband, depending on them each in turn to take the initiative. Never having lived my own life for even one year I feel I have missed out somewhere in my development."

No matter which role the twin plays in a dependency bond---the more assertive or the less---with the right person that twin can make a comfortable marriage. With the wrong mate, the potential for disaster is great, especially if the two new partners in marriage can't or won't tell each other what they each need. The expectations each of the newly weds bring into the marriage are crucial to its success. Many of these expectations turn out to be disastrously wrong.

Among the more fanciful expectations are those involving sexual curiosity. The sister who is a deadringer for her married twin invites speculation by the husband of her similarity in the nuptial bed. And same sisters also wonder about the man each has chosen. A few identical twin women who have a healthy sexual relationship with their husbands have candidly shared their awareness of their husband's fantasies of sharing both sisters in bed at the same time.

An identical twin from Ohio wrote to me on this subject.

"I know our husbands share the fantasy of having us both at the same time in their beds. It is fantasy that will never come true, but it is an entertaining one and a joke we can share. We know that sexual attitudes are formed by modeling our parent's behavior. We know our parents weren't too happy. We are hoping we formed some healthier attitudes along the way. One thing for sure, when we have compared notes on our sexual attitudes and have shared intimate details, some real bizarre similarities have emerged. No one taught us sex and she and I never really taught each other or discussed sexual likes or dislikes when we were engaged or newly married."

Another female twin wrote: "Once, the kids and I had gone on vacation and my husband and my twin were flying in from Los Angeles to meet us in Canada. They couldn't reach my vacation spot the same day so they stayed over night in a motel and slept in the same bed. This might sound kinky to the rest of the world, but to us it was just funny. My twin said she got worried when my husband threw his leg over her in the middle of the night. She pushed him gently, and said, "Bernie, dear, it's not Lou, it's me."

The expectations that can result in bitterness and eventual divorce are the unconscious ones in which a twin is convinced that his new mate will possess many of his twins' qualities and traits and

112

will be as alert to his private feelings as was the twin with whom he shared a biological destiny and a life time of adjustment.

As one twin I know said, "There was and still is a closeness with my twin that I never had with another person, not even my husband. She knows how I feel without having to explain."

The question of expectations in marriage leads naturally into the subject of why twins choose who they do for mates, and why are they chosen? The subject is a fascinating one that is certainly not exclusive with twins. The pleasant conundrum posed by the declaration, "Oh, I've just met the girl of my dreams," is the universal cry of mystery that stirs the imagination of every man or woman who has ever dreamed of love and a mate.

Investigators who study lives of twins are convinced that there are biological and psychological forces at work in the selection process by which a twin falls in love. But it is interesting to note, based on the statistics of the rates of celibacy among twins, that twins seem to have more resistance to marriage than singletons. What remains to be worked out is why.

Actually, we've already explored some important clues. Unreal expectations are a major one.

Doctor Charlotte Taylor who has done some remarkable research into the marriages of identical twins suggests that some expectations are based in the genetic code that twins share:

"Similarity in brain waves and in body build are proposed by certain scientists to be associated with more harmonious relationships. Two findings...give support to the idea that similarity at the chemical level may promote congeniality. First, many identical twins are extremely attached to each other. About three fourths of the twins in my study (of identical twins in marriage) have been living together in the same house even after having a family, and many of the remaining couples live next door to their twins or

113

within walking distance. The close ties between identical twins seem likely to be related to the similarity in their chemical makeup and hence in their temperament..."

Dr. Taylor points out the a molecular blue print in twins may indeed guide their marriage decisions:

"It has been known from previous research that identical twins have similar propensities for marriage, even if they have been raised apart in different home environments. Usually, both stay single, or both get married, or both get a divorce, or both get a series of divorces. Thus, I expected that identical twins married to identical twins would be likely to have an identical outcome of their marriages, and, as already noted, this was the case with all 50 couples I studied.

This fact is consistent with my contention of the overriding importance of physical and mental health in marriage, for identical twins have the same 'molecular blueprint' (genetic code) for physical and mental health."

A summary of Dr. Taylor's study of identical twins in quartenary marriages revealed that of 25 identical twin couples, overwhelmingly each couple acted as a unit in their marriage. Of four married persons if one of the two unions succeeded, the other did also. If one failed, so did the other. Twenty-two of the 25 marriages had long-terms success rates. That is an extraordinarily high result compared to the general population.

If there is a message in the success rate in these marriages for the rest of the world, twins and singletons, it is that biological and environmental similarities of twins to the twins they married are predominant factors. Good marriages may not be made in heaven, but they are inspired by the subtle, unconscious matching of traits that are dominant in each twin.

It seems fitting to end this chapter on marriage with the

114

shrewd observation by Alice Vollmer in a 1986 article for Twins Magazine:

"Whether or not to embrace a wider world through marriage can be a hard choice for twins. Because most marriages include periods of stress and upheaval, commitment to the marriage and tolerant acceptance of one another are integral to a strong relationship---even more so when marriage is paired with twinship. If twins are too attuned to each other and spouses feel left out, the marriage and twinship can be hard to reconcile. However, when twins and spouses can adapt to the intricacies of their situation, their marriages are embellished with a double measure of friendship and affection."

CHAPTER VIII

Parallel Lives

There are two startling and subtle experiences shared by twins that come closer than any others to defining the question, "We are twins but who am I ?" Parallelism and extrasensory perception in the lives of identical twins demonstrate a psychic relationship which is far from being understood. The whole idea of direct mental communication-----telepathy---of two minds so attuned that they are, " human echoes" of one another is disturbing to ordinary people, despite mounting evidence that clairvoyance may be a universal trait.

Arlene Mencke, a 66- year -old identical twin who lives in Eugene, Oregon, expressed the amazement that twins have about their psychic abilities when she said, "Often, my sister and I have had the same dream on the same night. I've had uncanny knowledge that something good or bad has happened to her when we were apart. We bought exactly the same gift for someone else, even to style and color, and we have given each other the same gift."

A 59- year- old California identical woman who lives an ocean apart from her sister wrote that, "Even though we have gone our separate ways, we have followed almost identical careers, life styles, tastes, even illnesses. It was marvelous, as I look back, that we shared everything, even when apart.

Her sister, who lives in Berkshire, England, concurred and said: "Four years ago I decided after much deliberation to resign from the job I was doing. Quite unknown to me my sister had made the same decision regarding her job. So we both changed jobs at the same time without even consulting or notifying the other. "

Many of the twins who took part in my survey are separated from their twin, yet it was remarkable how closely many of their answers matched on my questionaire. Marlene Follett, 46, of Tucson, Arizona noted that she and her twin "...lived in different states. We have purchased the same dress (while apart). We put the same shelf paper in our cupboards. When we get together we find we are wearing the same color of lipstick. Our seventh grade teacher separated us in class because she thought we were copying. After being separated we would still give the same answers on our work."

Marlene's twin, Charlene Dorman, who lives in California, answered the same question in the following way: "When we visit we find we have bought things just alike such as makeup, dresses, swimsuits, shelf paper. It's fun to see what the next thing will be."

In their book, *The Curious World Of Twins*, Vincent and Margaret Gaddis, suggested that twins who possess psychic abilities, "....may be able to identify chains of telepathic perception consciously, and there may be a steady flow of information, influence or sensation." The authors gave the example of young female twins who woke up screaming. They had been experiencing the same nightmare of walking along the edge of a cliff and then falling.

Strange psychic incidents contributing to parallel lives go on and on, often more spectacularly in twins who do not grow up together. Researchers in the famous Minnesota Twin Study found incredible parallels in the lives of identical twins who were separated at birth and reared without the knowledge that they had a twin.

Remarkable though the Minnesota study, led by Dr. Thomas Bouchard, has been, offering evidence that identical twins receive as much as 50 percent of their personality traits-----their composite character---from inherited genes, many twin researchers question whether the effect of heredity can be carved in granite. Says Susan Farber, a specialist in child development and assistant professor of clinical psychology at New York State University, who wrote *Identical Twins Reared Apart, A Reanalysis*, "The important thing to study is development (of twins). The most significant issue---and the one that will best explain some of the uncanny similarities in separated identical twins---- is how, and how much , genetic constitution influences each child's progress through the development process."

What Farber has said strikes at the base reason for the continuing study of twins, identicals especially. She has pointed out that genes switch on and off, sometimes as a direct response to environment, sometimes as a result of the effects of environment filtering through the physiological process.

"What we need to examine," she states, "...is the blueprint of development and how it is modified by genetic and environmental influences. Only then will we begin to understand cognition as opposed to I. Q. test scores, or personality as opposed to a list of particular traits."

Intriguing, and prophetic for twins and for all human beings is the idea contained in Farber's concluding statement for an article in Psychology Today: "Once we begin to understand how genes and environment interact in the organization and reorganization of personality , we may begin to understand something that is really worth knowing."

Of course, this statement reflects the reason for studying the parallelism in the lives of twins. Such evidence provides researchers and ultimately all of us, with a base of reliable reference against which to measure ourselves and to discover our potential for unlimited mental enlargement and spiritual growth. The sooner we can identify the barriers to stretching ourselves that heredity and environment impose, the sooner we can release the genius of our true selves.

The ongoing study by the Minnesota Center for Twins and Adoption Research of the University of Minnesota, has subjected 106 sets of twins from the U.S. , Great Britian, and other countries, to more physical and psychological scrutiny than most of us experience in a lifetime. Sixty-five percent of the twins are identical. In the course of a week, twin pairs are x-rayed fingerprinted, heart-monitored, tested for intelligence, and questioned on everything from their sex lives, to their work histories, to their fears and phobias.

The Minnesota Study is by far the largest in depth twin study ever. But of greatest fascination are the program's 55 pairs of identical twins who were separated shortly after birth(usually given up for adoption), reared apart and reunited in adulthood.

While we've always known we can inherit physical characteristics from our biological parents, the Minnesota findings showed that even personality traits are highly influenced by genetic factors. Indeed, among identical twins, such common traits as cheerfulness, confidence, and caution are found to be determined more by inheritance than by upbringing.

Some researchers have theorized that identical twins inherit a bio-chemical communication system that allows them to send and receive impressions from below the threshhold of normal perception. One of the proponents of " macrophages" communication was Dr. Hilda G. Heine who in her book *The Vital Sense:The Implications and Exploitation of The Sixth Sense*, explained the organization of tiny amoeboid cells which are "the physiological and real part of the soul." They are the sense organ of the sixth sense, she claimed, "a very elusive kind of sense organ, " which is more sensitive in some than others.

Dr. Heine believed that in early childhood the activity of the macrophages system is most pronounced. As a consequence, young children are particularly adept at picking up emanations and vibrations from others. "Since the contact between twins is particularly close," she wrote, "one would assume them to be knit by a very efficient telepathic system and there is evidence to confirm this."

There are many other attractive theories to account for the psychic phenomena between twins, and which of them emerges as the most reliable remains for the researchers to prove. The fact remains that identical twins are the living laboratories that provide us with unique information about psychic communication. We are learning through their experiences what powers lie ahead of us--- what we dimly perceive as astonishing new adventures for the mind and spirit.

One of the most tragic and bewildering set of twins who practiced a form of telepathic communication characterized by one of the twins as, "She is the ghost and I am the mortal soul, " was a strange, doomed relationship between Jennifer and June Gibbons. Described in the book *The Silent Twins*, author Marjorie Wallace said of the two girls who grew up in Wales, "Like twin stars, they are caught up in a gravitational field between them, doomed to spin around each other forever. If they come too close or drift apart, both are destroyed."

Terrified and compelled by their paradoxical fascination and attraction to one another, the girls were willing participants in sex, marijuana, liquor, glue sniffing and wilder and wilder escapades of burglary and arson, thrilling each other and bolstering the paired psychic intelligence that represented their separate but intertwined minds.

Their eventual arrest and indefinite confinement in Broadmoor, which is the most notorious maximum security hospital in Britain, brought to an incomplete solution the bizarre drama of their convoluted personalities which became twisted like two incestuous snakes writhing and looping together in tight endless spasms of secret excitement and shuddering sensation.

Their tragedy is that they became not a couple but a "double" fascinated and transfixed by their simultaneity.

Most twins who connect by extrasensory perception demonstrate singular episodes of clairvoyance. In her book, *Twins:Nature's Amazing Mystery*, Kay Cassill wrote about two Indiana girls who had "sixth sense qualities," according to their father.

One night Stella burned her hand with an iron while she was pressing clothes and in the same instant was overcome by a feeling of terror, dizziness, and nausea. When the attack passed she rushed to a carnival which her sister, Della, was attending. She felt compelled to go. When Stella arrived, she discovered her twin was trapped in a car stalled on top of the Ferris wheel. Terrified, she was

121

swaying back and forth.

When Della was rescued, she rushed into her sister's arms and said, "Stella won't you ever learn how to iron? You burned yourself again."

There was no conceivable way in which either of the girls could have communicated with each other, yet Stella knew her sister was in trouble on the damaged Ferris wheel, and Della knew Stella had burned her hand while ironing.

Ann Race, 39, who lives in Charleston, Massachusetts told me of an experience she shared with her sister that was also astonishing.

"I went to have my ears pierced in high school and Lou came along for the ride. She was sitting in the doctor's waiting room and when I walked out of the office after that painful experience, I looked at Lou and her ears were as red as beets." Ann's sister, Lou, had actually experienced the psychic reenactment of her sister's pain at the moment the Doctor pierced Ann's ears.

Even stranger was the experience of Kim and Kyle Richardson both of whom were playing golf on the sameday on July 13, 1988. The twin brothers were 2,000 miles apart, however---Kim at Indian Springs Golf Course, Silver Springs, Maryland, Kyle at Grand Lake Golf Course, Grand Lake, Colorado---when they both made eagles at 2 P.M. exactly! Both used 7-irons from the ninth hole, shooting 410 yards to make par-4.

Said Louise LaCroix, who lives in Bellevue, Washington, "My twin and I have had many ESP experiences. We often get sick at the same time and our highs and lows generally correspond. We often buy the same clothes by accident, and a mutual friend reported that she received a letter from each of us on the same day."

Another identical woman told me, " We end up wearing the same outfits when neither of us knows what the other is wearing.

This amazes people we are traveling with. We go to the doctor for the same things. Our doctor knows when one of us goes to him that he will see the other one in a week or two."

Jack Springer, 32, of Portland, Oregon, believes that he and his sister share ESP. He reported: "We seem to be able to tell when something is wrong with one another. Sometimes we think or say the same things. When we were in the seventh grade, my sister came down with a kidney disease and almost died. I felt so helpless, I wanted to do something to help her. I was hit by a car on my bike on my way home for lunch. That night when my parents went to see my sister she knew something terrible had happened to me. I was on the floor above her at the hospital. Eerie huh."

Fascinated with such true incidents in the lives of twins, Dr. Stanley Krippner, a dream researcher at Maimonides Medical Center in Brooklyn, New York, has engaged in controlled dream experiments with twins and is convinced as a result of the demonstrations by twins of sending and receiving dreams that there are wide implications to telepathy.

"It's my hunch," he was reported saying in *The Curious World Of Twins*, by Vincent and Margaret Gaddis, "that we'll eventually have to reverse our image of man, on the basis of telepathic evidence. At present, psychology views each person as an alienated man, cut off from his surroundings, basically alone.

"Telepathy may teach us that in the basic fabric of life everything and everyone is linked, that man is continuously enmeshed, that he is always and integral part of life on the face of the earth."

The single most challenging aspect of the various researches----the Minnesota study being foremost----of similarities of separated identical twins is the concept of simultaneity in pair after pair who have been studied. Almost like carbon copies of one another, the identicals have reported strikingly similar life styles and preferences, from wives with the same name, to the same model and color of car to the same brand of cigarettes.

Why have the identical twins studied who had the least opportunity for mutual intelligence turn out the most alike, while those with the greatest opportunity for mutual identification moved in opposite directions?

From my survey one answer may lie in the complex interaction known as twining, a process that occurs when twins are raised together. When families have identical twins, they may treat them in subtly different ways, probably without consciously intending to do so, in an attempt to differentiate between them. For example, if one of the pair is more adept physically, the parents may designate one as, "the athlete", while the less active one becomes, "the thinker".

The twins themselves, as we know from observation and from their own reports, seesaw between close identification with each other and exaggerated independence. If one does well in science, the other may map out territory elsewhere, simply out of a need for individuality.

Thus, as other investigators have also suggested, it is possible that being reared with a twin overshadows genetic tendencies to grow up alike. But when twins are reared apart and the potential twining interaction cannot occur, then, perhaps, genetic predispositions show themselves more forcefully.

These observations seem to be born out by twins like Tony Milasi, of Binghampton, New York, and Roger Williams of Miami, Florida.

Certainly stranger than fiction, the true story of the boys represents a classic case of separated----and reunited identicals.

The boys were born out of wedlock in Binghampton, a small

city in upstate New York, on May 28th, 1938. Father of the boys was a Jewish pots and pan salesman who came calling on an attractive young woman who became their mother, Marie, an Italian Catholic who was home alone when she opened the door to Jules Brooks.

Their affair resulted in twins which neither Jules, who was married, and Marie, also married with children, wanted. They were able to arrange the adoption of one twin(Tony) with Pauline Milasi. The second unchosen twin was shunted from one foster home to another.

In one home a parent dropped a lighted cigarette into Roger's crib and the baby was burned along his left side. To this day he carries the scars.

Four years after he was burned, a remarkable thing happened. Mrs. Mildred Brooks, the wife of Jules, the biological father, learned of her spouse's infidelity and insisted on adopting the still homeless twin, Roger. Later when her marriage failed, Mildred and her mother moved to Florida, taking with them Mildred's adopted son Roger.

Now the living laboratory was in place. Tony lived in the North, an altar boy at mass, a lackadaisical student and a teenage enlistee in the Navy. In the South, Roger was a struggling schoolboy in Miami, a favorite in a Rabbi's home and a teen-age enlistee in the Air Force.

Did either of the boys have an inkling that there was a missing half of himself? If so, the haunting didn't surface until a busboy at a pancake house brought the young men together when they were both 24. Roger was identified as the double for Tony in Binghampton, New York.

The deliberately low-key reunion was held in Miami, but

shortly thereafter Roger moved to Binghampton to be near Tony.

Talk about similarities! When Roger and Tony got together they discovered both brushed their teeth with an unusual Swedish toothpaste called Vademecum, and each used the same aftershave lotion and the same hair dressing.

Among female identicals who have reported parallel lives and telepathic communications are Candi and Randi Brough, 24-year-olds who starred in the TV sitcom *B.J. and The Bear* several years ago. According to the girls , they have shared a closer bond then identicals because they are what physicians call, "mirror-image-twins." To my knowledge there is no evidence that mirror-image twins exhibit a closer bond than other identicals.

Children born with this designation generally demonstrate clock-wise and counter-clock-wise swirls of the hair, right-handedness and left-handedness.

Randi said ,"Doctors have told us that mirror-image-twins are closer than identicals because the egg had waited longer to separate. They are almost one being.

"Looking at Candi is like looking in the mirror because I am right-handed and she is left-handed. Candi's handwriting slants to the left and mine to the right, so if you put a piece of paper with my handwriting on it up to a mirror it would be identical to Candi's."

According to an article by Robin Leech in *Star Magazine*, the amazing similarity of the women helped the young actresses to survive when they moved to Hollywood looking for their big break in show business.

Candi explained: "We could only afford to move into an apartment where one person was allowed to live. The management was very strict about this rule and in order to fool them we always left the apartment at separate times. "

"We felt bad about having to fool the landlady, but we

couldn't afford two separate places."

The blue-eyed twins who both measure five feet four inches and weigh 97 pounds each, have an astonishing psychic bond. They share the same thoughts, said Randi. "Often Candi will start a sentence and I will finish the thought."

"We even share dreams. As we grew up we always shared the same dreams and nightmares on the same night. It was very strange because everything in the dreams from beginning to end would be the same."

Though not mirror-image-twins, Lorna Albrecht of Harrisburg, Pennsylvania, and her sister Gloria Frank of the same city, have shared sympathetic feelings while apart that once again demonstrate a sensitivity to one another that is striking.

Lorna wrote to me to say that she had had a hysterectomy in 1976. On the day of her operation her sister's menstrual period stopped. Each time Lorna had babies her sister went into false labor and it was later discovered she began at the same instant Lorna's birthing pains started..

Nancy Segal, one of the Minnesota Twin Project's investigators, sent me the story of two identical twins who were united 31 years after they were adopted out to different families following their births. The bizarre story of lives apart and their union at which they discovered amazing similarities presents another case to demonstrate the importance of heredity in shaping personality, as opposed to the argument that environment is the major influence in the formation of an individual.

The story Nancy sent me related that Mark Newman and Jerald Levy, members respectively of the Paramus volunteer fire department in New Jersey and of the Wayside Fire Department in Tinton Falls, New Jersey, discovered one another as the result of another fireman,Captain Jim Tedesco, who was convinced that a lookalike he met at a state convention was related to a fireman in his own company.

Tedesco convinced Mark Newman to travel to Tinton Falls to look at some new fire equipment, convinced he would never make the trip if he were asked to believe that he might have a twin brother.

When Newman arrived at the firehouse his overriding interest was to see the new apparatus Tedesco had promised.

When he got out of the car and walked into the firehouse, he passed right by Jerry Levy, then remarked to Tedesco, "Where's the foam unit? This is nothing but a pumper."

Tedesco said, "Mark, come over here and look at this firefighter. Doesn't he look a little familiar to you?"

Mark stopped and looked at Jerry. "You're right," he said "---has a nose like me...He wears glasses like me...He's bald like me..."

Stunned, the twin firefighters walked in front of a mirror, gaped at the images they saw, and then let out a shout.

Aside from displaying the matching genetic features they were born with, the double image showed Levy and Newman that they even groomed themselves in the same way. Both sported sideburns and moustaches of equal length and with a similar curl, both wore metalframed aviator type eye glasses. Their mannerisms were alike, their voices were indistinguishable, their gaits identical. Said Newman: "Every time we did something it seemed to be in unison. That's when it really started to get scary."

The firefighters initial meeting was the beginning of a close friendship that united their adoptive families and revealed even more parallels, and dissimilarities in their lives.

Both men are bachelors and both enjoy fishing, hunting, motorcycling, eating Italian food, and going to the beach. And , both have an intense interest in firefighting.

How do they explain that even their smallest, most trivial actions are the same? "We are cloneheads," said Levy. "Even our baby pictures are alike-----we are wearing the same shirts, the crew-cuts, the same facial expressions . And now I feel I have lived with Mark for 31 years."

Identical twins who have been separated like Mark and Jerry represent the controversy that stirs researchers to heated discussion and strong argument. Heretofore, the view of social scientists has rested firmly upon the notion that environment is the single most potent factor in the formation of personality. To arrive at this understanding, environmental behaviorists had to live down the famous study of twins that became notorious because of its fraudulent perceptions.

Twin research is still recovering from the English psychologist Cyril Burt. Burt used his twin studies to advance his theory that intelligence is largely inherited. "Genes are 87 percent responsible for I.Q.", he claimed,"while environmental factors account for 13 percent."

"Since intelligence is overwhelmingly inborn ," Burt argued, "superior ability will show itself over any environmental conditions-------no matter how impoverished."

On the basis of Burt's studies, a universal I.Q. test was administered to every English schoolchild who reached age 11. The child's educational future rested on those test scores------he was either on to a university program, or into a trade school, and sometimes back to the streets. The tracked school system instituted under Burt's influence lasted from 1938 to 1967 when it was abandoned.

Meanwhile, Burt retired, living a quiet life in London. But increasingly,his ideas came under fire until five years after his death his own records revealed that he had lied, had fabricated some of the data he had used to support his theory of heredity as a governing factor in human personality.

The alleged fraud cast a shadow of suspicion on twin studies and gave a clear field to proponents of the environmental theory of personality influence. But today the study of twins raised apart is now gaining world-wide attention as the result of the Minnesota program.

The findings of the Minnesota program have rekindled an old and bitter debate over heredity. Its conclusion fly in the face of the environmental theories which had been the basis of many political programs that seek to reverse the social causes of property and crime.

David Lykken, a University of Minnesota psychologist closely involved in the twins project, plays down the debate. "This is not war," he said in a *U.S. News and World Report* article. "Part of our study is simply replicating what has already been proven. We are just showing it with a larger number of twins, and, with those who are raised apart."

According to the same article, the real controversy stems from another part of the study-----which says the same environment affects people differently, that common experiences do not create common personality traits. "That", says Lykken, "makes a lot of people nervous."

One of the people who have disagreed with Lykken's conclusions has been Leon Kamin, professor of psychology at Princeton and co-author of *Not In Our Genes*, who calls the Minnesota study not only "irresponsible", but ," flat wrong."

"It will be used, " he said, "to argue that you can't throw money at problems, that human behavior is determined by genes and there's nothing we can do about it. This has nothing to do with science. It's a political debate."

But Lykken insists that the kind of genetic research being conducted at the University of Minnesota is supportive of social intervention. And that parents are not fully powerless to shape the development of their children. A hypothetical case that he used to demonstrate his point was ace test pilot Chuck Yagger who may have been born daring. The point Lykkens made was that if Yagger had had overprotective parents who kept him from jumping off barns, he might never have grown up to be the first aviator to break the sound barrier.

Despite the mild furor over the supremacy of nature or nurture as a philosophical basis upon which to judge the actions of humans, the fact remains that the most encouraging outcome of studies such as the Minnesota Project is the eye it gives to all of us to gaze at broader human horizons.

I like what dream researcher Dr. Stanley Krippner said when he proposed that telepathy (between twins) may teach us that all living things are linked in a basic fabric of life. Isn't it grand and remarkable that the biological accident of being a twin may produce information that could lead to such a profound and suitable explanation of the arrangement of life--------and eventually to its purpose?

131

CHAPTER IX

Loss Of A Twin

Of all the human relationships recorded, none are so extraordinary as the ones between identical twins who are parted by death. Several cases have been documented in which a twin, sensing the inevitable death of his stricken twin, has decided to die simultaneously. "Dying to stay together" is rare among the thousands of twins who are separated by death. Far more common are "linked-life" experiences that demonstrate how traumatic and disorienting to the survivor the loss of his twin can be.

In case after case, surviving twins have told of a prescient feeling, a strange uneasiness, a sense of something about to happen, just before their twin was fatally injured or died of an illness. Other twins have expressed a terrible draining away of themselves, a sense of sharp displacement so acute that they have confused the identity

132

of who has died, themselves or their twin.

A Minnesota identical twin, Mona, told of staring at her dead twin lying in her coffin and reaching out to touch her hand. At the moment of contact, Mona said she felt a strange shock go through her and she remembered seeing her own hand become "hazy", as if it was fading away. A few days later in her room looking at herself and her hand in a mirror, Mona started trembling with severe shock. She had the weird feeling that it was she, not her sister, who was dead and the figure in the mirror was not a reflection of herself.

So severe was the feeling of separation from herself that Mona sought psychiatric help at a mental health center. For weeks she received therapeutic counseling, the doctor instructing her to continue to reassure herself that "When you look in the mirror know that you are looking at yourself and your hand, not your sister and her hand."

Mona required several months of therapy until she adjusted from a double life to a single one. There were many times during the period of her counseling that she was not sure who was dead. Her appearance before a mirror brought on terrible spasms and her body would shake. Eventually , she moved to New York, taking a job as a housekeeper at a hospital.

When Mona wrote to me she expressed the hope that the telling of her experience would be helpful to other twins going through the process of adjusting to the death of a twin, the death of part of themselves.

Karrie Bettes of Ashland, Oregon knows what it is to receive a premonition about a twin. She and her identical twin sister,Kathy, were having coffee together on Friday, November 11, 1983. They loved to have long talks about old times, friends they shared and their children. Meeting together was a comfortable ritual that both women enjoyed and anticipated. The sisters were particularly close, drawn together to comfort one another after the death of their mother when they were 14.

When Karrie and Kathy finished their coffee and started to leave the restaurant, a strong feeling of dismay came over Karrie. She stared at Kathy suddenly, trying to find a clue to her own apprehension in her sister's face. Something was wrong, but Karrie didn't know what. Reluctantly, she parted with Kathy, pushing aside the uneasiness she felt.

Less than an hour after Karrie had arrived home from the restaurant, she received an urgent call from Kathy's husband.

"Kathy's been in an accident," he said.

Karrie rushed to her car and drove madly to the hospital. She learned Kathy had been in a freeway accident and was in critical condition. Her blood pressure was dangerously low, and ten minutes later her heart stopped beating.

After Kathy's death, Karrie tried to avoid going places where her sister had been known.   Being mistaken for Kathy hurt Karrie deeply, reminding her of the depth of her loss.

The mental rapport between some identical twins is so astonishing that it has been labeled as a form of clairvoyance. If that explanation is unsatisfactory it is because thought transference is unsubstantiated scientifically. Also, nobody really understands how clairvoyance works, much less the sense of "halfing", the sudden loss of identity many twins describe when death separates them from their twin. No one knows for certain how thought passes between one person and another. The enigma is fascinating and so are identical twins to ESP researchers because they are the ones who have demonstrated the most extraordinary facility in the exchange of unspoken thoughts.

Parents are perplexed and awed by routine mental exchanges

between identical twins who may be separated by thousands of miles:

A mother of identical twin sons reported that Harvey nonchalantly told her one day that his brother, Harry, had won a swimming meet at the YMCA.

"How do you know that?" she asked him.

He just shrugged.

"He knew Harry had won before he came home to show me his medal."

Another parent reported her teen-age daughter's sudden anxiety one evening. The 14- year-old jumped up from her chair and said positively, "Chandra's been hurt, I think she's broken her wrist."

The identical twin sister was spending the night at a friend's house at a slumber party. A few minutes after Chandra's sister warned that she'd been hurt, the mother of Chandra's friend telephoned to report that Chandra had been taken to the hospital with a broken wrist, suffered when the girls had gotten too rambunctious in the bedroom.

In his book, *Linked Lives*, author Harvey Day reported that twin dancers Jean and Joe Readinger both thought up the identical original dance routine while one was in Chicago and the other was in Pittsburgh. They danced the complicated steps together when they were reunited just as if they had been practicing the routine together for months.

There is very little research on ESP in twins. One of the explanations offered for the paucity of material is that ESP----embracing telepathy, clairvoyance, psychokinesis----does not have enough credibility as a science or discipline of study to attract money to pay for investigators.

This was summarized by Nancy L. Segal, twin research

135

associate in the Department of Psychology at the University of Minnesota, when she wrote "...little progress has been made toward confirming the presence of ESP between twins. Few studies have been attempted and fewer still have found evidence of the phenomenon."

Lack of overwhelming evidence does not change the fact that twin observers who have collected impressive amounts of anecdotal data on psychic transactions between twins are completely convinced of their reliability. They predict that twins who exhibit supersensory communication will open the door to a deeper understanding of thought transference despite the lack of scientific study in the field.

A striking incident demonstrates the strong psychic bond that exists between some twins. In some cases it is so strong that it may precipitate a death signal that both twins may share simultaneously.

Loy Henderson, former United States Ambassador to India, Iran and Iraq, reported a vision in which his brother, Roy, appeared by his bedside while Loy was lying in a hospital convinced he was near death. Loy and his brother talked of the pain of their parting, then Roy disappeared. Instead of dying, Loy recovered and three days later a cablegram was delivered which announced his brother's death---of an infection following a tooth extraction, at the same instant he had appeared in his brother's farewell vision at the hospital.

If some twins can share ordinary thoughts, can duplicate ideas, emulate one another's choices of colors, clothes, cars, and choose marriage partners with the same name, even dream alike simultaneously, imagine then the shock to the survivor of the death of a twin. The sense of deprivation may be so fundamental that it may penetrate into the remaining twin's deepest subconscious levels

136

of self awareness. The shock may prove too severe for the survivor to live.

The grief of an identical twin for his absent "other half" goes far beyond the normal sense of loss. It involves the emptiness that results from the destruction of the "couple effect". This phenomenon was identified by Rene Zazzo of the University of Paris who has been studying twin patterns. Zazzo concluded that traditional methods of studying twins were in error by regarding them as doubles rather than as "couples".

"Only a few of the remarkable peculiarities of twins' development are known for sure," Zazzo observed, "such as delayed intellectual development, language retardation...difficulties related to fragile self-consciousness and sociability."

As a result of Zazzo's concept of two as a couple, other twin researchers began to see that twins had created a priority in their understanding of their own true identities. *Ourselves* came before *myself*. Identical twins, especially, think of themselves as one unit, rather than as two persons who look and act alike. This couple definition was buttressed by the science of Chronogenetics which has discovered that some identical twins are fated by their inherited genes to die at the same time of the same disease.

John and Arthur Mowforth, former Royal Air Force pilots who died of heart attacks within the same hour on May 4, 1975, are but one example of dozens of the stunning coincidence of the couple effect in death.

Given the time clock in the genes of many identical twins, and the social, psychological, environmental and psychic dual development of identical twins, it seems apparent that the separation that death brings between the "couple" who are twins is not only shocking to the surviving twin, but actually feels to him as if his body and soul have been severed.

137

I received a touching letter from Jerry Zimmer of Farmington, Minnesota in January 1991 which sensitively expressed grief, disorientation, pathos and the physical and psychic yearning through which Jerry passed since his brother, Jim, died. The letter is printed here with Jerry's permission:

On December 8, 1985 at 12:39 P.M., my twin was killed in a plane crash. At the same time I was ice skating with my two older boys. I discovered later that at the same instant he was killed my body went into a wave of awful shock.

I instantly ached from head to toe from an awful pain like, maybe, being under a 20-ton pile of rock. I felt like I was being crushed from the outside in. The intensity of this physical discomfort was the same in my eyelids as on my back and toes. It is hard to describe the feeling. Being crushed is as close as I can come to describing it. My voice totally disappeared. I could not talk. I tried, but my vocal cords would not respond to my mental command. This , is too hard to explain.

It was like being mute. My mouth moved but no sound came out. Days passed before I could talk and many times when I was speaking my voice would suddenly disappear.

Those pains of grief lasted on and off for over three years. Even today, I have them and when I think about Jim my voice goes away. Five years after his death, I have adjusted to the crush pain and voice loss. When it comes it doesn't last very long and it doesn't happen very often.

After Jim's death my memory became very good. I could recall our whole life together, every little detail from childhood to being 40 years old. Even today, my memory of Jim and our life together is totally recallable.

Jim and I were, and still are, best friends. A best friend is a person you can share your most private thoughts with, and he or she can appreciate things spouses can't. They can't share thoughts like identical twins do. Spouses and offspring aren't as good a friend as a twin.

Never a night or day goes by that I don't think of Jim. I have not had a good night's sleep in five years. He is always at the threshold of my conscious mind. When I meditate and communicate with him, I think I hold both sides of our conversation because I know what he is going to say to me. We never have stopped talking to each other.

When Jim and I were alive we worked out all of our problems, big and little together. Now I battle them alone.

After his death I contemplated suicide thousands of times. I pleaded and prayed to God to take me too. I wanted to be with Jim more than I wanted to live. Those feelings are still with me after five years of his being gone.

It took four of those five years to come to the reality that Jim was really gone. Thousands of times I would pinch myself or slap myself trying to wake up from the awful dream of his death. I couldn't believe he was really gone.

I have no close or good friend now, and probably never will. I deeply want my oldest boy to be a little like Jim but he isn't old enough yet to understand my loss.

The worst thing about Jim being gone is, I have no one to share my thoughts with and my grief. As for how to prepare for a loss like this, I don't know what to do.

Twins seeking consolation and understanding for the long period of grieving and sense of abandonment they feel when they lose a twin have found relief talking with other twins. These veterans of loss realize the death of a twin does not change the relationship for the survivor. Some moving testimony has been recorded by surviving twins who insist they will not allow death to force them to relinquish the distinction of being a twin. They consider themselves to be "separated" twins that will be reunited with their missing twin at some point in the future after their own death.

Dr. Raymond W. Brandt of Fort Wayne, Indiana---founder of the Twinless Twins Support Group of the International Twins Association--beautifully expressed the confidence of the surviving twin in the ultimate reunion when he wrote:

"I remember distinctly how I knew the exact moment when my twin was accidentally electrocuted on an electric transmission line pole. A strange, indescribable feeling overwhelmed me. I knew my twin's soul had left his physical body and my soul felt like joining his. I yearned to be with him where he had gone, but my life on earth continued on. When my death does come, I know I will not be disappointed. I will be on my merry way to join my identical twin---join myself as it were, and become a wholeness once again."

The loss of a twin also affects other members of the family in a different way than the death of a child who is a singleton. Much of the adjustment to the loss will depend on how the twins related to one another and to other members of the family. Age of the twin at death is also a major factor.

Because of the burden of grief and the decisions that have to be made at the time of death parents often fail to assist the surviving twin with his emotions. Involved in their own hurt, they forget the remaining twin's deeper anguish. He can suffer two losses as a result of his twin's demise---the loss of his twin, obviously, and, temporarily, the support of his parents.

Each parent develops an individual relationship with a

140

child, and each parent will react to the loss in a different way. This may lead to marital strain if the mother and the father fail to meet the other's expectation for grief or support. This family strain will certainly affect the surviving twin.

If the parents have made "twin parenthood" an essential part of their own self image and have difficulty adjusting to the idea of one instead of "the couple", the surviving twin may see himself as having little worth as a single child. This can be a difficult time for him. He may feel excluded from his parent's grief, particularly if they act as if grieving is a silent, personal affair and never talk about the lost twin, or remove all evidence of his existence, creating a ghost.

In this case,the surviving twin cannot express his own grief, guilt or anger. He may even interpret his parents actions as a silent accusation of blame for his twin's death. Unless he can get help to resolve his feelings, he may carry his twin's ghost well into adulthood.

Parents often fear that they also will lose their surviving child. This is particularly acute if the twins were young, or if the ailment was one that had a genetic base. Parents may become overprotective and give the surviving twin the message that life is full of danger. The twin may become timid and afraid of any physical or emotional separation from his mother and father. Interdependence may interfere with the formation of other relationships, especially with the opposite sex. Some children may react to this unhealthy parental smothering by openly defying danger and inviting parental punishment.

Seeking to replace the lost twin by transferring all of their expectations for the lost child onto his surviving twin, can also be devastating for that remaining twin. Encouraged to live for two , the survivor may take on some personality traits of his lost twin. He may also try to fill the empty place by engaging in activities in which his twin excelled.

The other factor that would affect the parents' grief and the actions of the surviving twin are the circumstances of the death. If the death was sudden, the surviving twin may identify with the pain and try to relive the event in his nightmares. Possibly, he may feel guilty that he survived or that he was not able to prevent the accident. The way in which the surviving twin reacts to the death of his twin will depend on how close the two were.

Children under five usually have very little understanding of death and what it means. The surviving twin may insist on taking his brother's place. He may sit at the table where his brother sat or take over his teddy bear or other toys. He may carry on conversations with his dead twin and include him with his drawings of the family. Often the surviving twin even fantasizes about his own death as a way of finding his lost brother or sister.

In an article in *Twins Magazine* Sheryl McInnis observed that "Parents must be very careful about how they discuss death. If it is glorified, or if the child is told that when he dies he will join his twin, they may be laying the ground for an attempted suicide. One mother noted that for a few months after his twin died, her son did everything he could to put himself in danger. When she drew his attention to what the consequences might be if he was not more careful, he would reply that it didn't matter because if he died he'd be with his brother and have someone to play with again."

According to McInnis, a young child may also display some personality changes such as becoming destructive or withdrawn.

Death is understood better, she noted, by the child as he matures and learns to put time in perspective and to develop his own sense of mortality. However, even children in their teens need to talk about their feelings. They may be experiencing the guilt of survival and now have a greater share of the parents attention.

McInnis points out that "The twin who has a solid sense of his separate self will feel the loss as profoundly as one who does not, but the more mature twin may be able to work through the grieving process with less lasting pain than the twin with little or no separate identity."

Twins who have experienced the loss of a twin themselves can offer invaluable support to a newly bereaved twin. It was put in perspective by Marion Hearn when he wrote to me about the loss of his identical twin brother, Melvin, of Stafford, Kansas. Following is an excerpt from his letter which he would like to share:

Some of the things I found difficult to contend with are like not having Melvin's helping hand and his part in making many decisions. Another is not being able to pick up the phone and call him or have him call me on our FM radio system. A vacant chair in the family circle on so many occasions, especially during the holidays of Thanksgiving, Christmas, and New Years, causes emptiness.

From time to time I have to tell myself that Melvin would be proud of me for what I have done or am doing. I realize now that when we lost other loved ones we had the support of each other. One thing our minister told me I will always remember is ""Hang onto your faith" ,and I'd sure pass that on to anyone else.

My faith in God, the strength in prayer and the power of positive thinking, the support of my wife, family and friends in the community ,are all a great support to me. I would suggest to anyone experiencing such a loss that at any time you feel like crying do so. Tears are words of love spoken from the bottom of our hearts.

Many times when I realize that I'm a little depressed I switch to the power of positive thinking and think how fortunate I have been having been a twin.

143

The adjustment to the death of a twin was eloquently described by James S. Wilson of Oklahoma City, Oklahoma in a letter to me. Jim's words are reprinted here with his permission. His message is one that will help assuage the grief of every twin who loses a twin.

We were born in 1951 and Bill died in 1985. Quite simply stated, this was by far the most devastating event in my life and will always be with the exception of my own death. No one understands the size of the loss. I quit talking about it to people long ago because they don't know how to relate to the loss of one so close.

A little background. Bill and I lived apart for most of our adult lives. He was single and I am in my second, and successful, marriage. We spoke on the phone several times a week and stayed in communication even if one or both of us were out of the country. We tried to visit each other three or more times each year.

My first wife was extremely jealous of our relationship but Nancy loved him like a brother. She did not pit us against one another like Jane did. To give you an idea of how close we were, I remember the day before he died he realized that he should eat something to maintain strength but could not think of anything that sounded good. Several visitors made suggestions but nothing worked. I took one look at him and said "ice cream" and he immediately perked up and told us that was the only thing.

About a week before his death, he was visiting us in Oklahoma City and we decided to go to a Tina Turner concert. I took my camera to get pictures but got caught with it at the gate. They did not allow photographic equipment inside the hall. I left to go back to the car while Nancy and Bill went inside to get seated. Nancy wondered why I was taking so long to return and Bill told her that I was trying to find a way to smuggle the camera past the gate. She disagreed with him saying that I would never do that. About five minutes later in I walked with a sweater over the camera. Nancy was amazed that someone else knew me better than she.

I won't go into much detail of the events surrounding Bill's death. He'd been sick off and on for years. When I learned of his final illness, we flew to see him not expecting him to die. The shock, no, terror, of seeing him lifeless on that hospital bed burned and unforgettable memory onto my brain. I was not prepared for the magnitude of this event.

We went about the task of funeral arrangements in one city and then shipping him to our hometown for another service and burial. Calling my parents that day was extremely difficult. I must have been on automatic pilot. The feeling was one of periods of numbness separated by stretches of reality with immense sorrow. I cried so much those days that I developed an ear infection that I still have today.

I believe I dealt with his loss as best as can be done given the situation. I was not immobilized for very long and I attribute that to several things I did most of which were not thought out ahead of time as one would in a pre-conceived plan to get through the grieving.

The arranging for the funeral and seeing him dead helped put a finality to his life. Speaking at his service in my hometown was very hard but helped me face the good of his life and recognize the end of it. I spoke because no one else that was to speak had known him like I did. I'm sure he would have appreciated the fact that I read a Catholic prayer (St. Francis of Asisi) in a Southern Baptist church. I talked of his love for life and the great things he did to help those in need around him. Few knew the vast amounts of time he gave to others with no expectation of anything in return.

Since Bill was single, Nancy and I cleaned out his apartment taking four days to do so. We went through everything, bills, keepsakes, closets, drawers, etc. We would find pictures and other reminders and laugh and cry. We sold what we could and took the rest home. It was a very grueling process but also a healing one.

Even as I write this letter to you, I find a measure of relief, which leads me to the most beneficial action I took, and that is to expressing myself verbally or in writing to a third party that really cares! At first Nancy was a tremendous help and so were my older brother and parents to a degree. But there was something big missing and feelings still were not addressed.

I went to an expensive psychologist and he helped some but I could tell that his interest was more at the financial level than at the soul. I could not seem to get the knack of going into the session calm and collected, express myself to a high level of emotion, and then fall back to "normal" in a fixed period of time, usually 45 minutes.

A few months after his death, I contacted the twin research team at Minnesota University. By chance I noticed an article in a magazine about the program at Minnesota. It talked briefly about their study of twin loss and I called to offer my help. My motivation was to offer my assistance but I was also looking for a way to fill the need I had ---the need to understand what had happened to me.

Dr. Nancy Segal returned my call and we had a good talk. I later filled out a survey on twin loss that she had sent. A few months later I met her in Oklahoma City at the annual twins convention. Dr. Brandt and others had founded a twin loss support group and this was to be the first meeting. The group met but I found the meeting very inadequate other than it was comforting to know that others had experienced my same loss. The group was named "Twinless Twins" after my suggestion.

I found the meeting lacking in that everyone had so many unexpressed feelings and emotions that a one hour meeting each

146

year was like a drop in the ocean. It was clear to me all of us required one-on-one sessions with a professional or one of the other members of the group.

Nancy Segal and I met for over an hour after the meeting and I came away from that talk a different person. She had so many good things to say as well as knew how to listen. I believed her when she said that some questions had no answers. Her combined experience as a twin, trained psychologist, and twin expert, along with a genuine caring helped that missing feeling go away. In the five years after his death it has not returned.

Nancy and I have stayed in touch although I am long overdue to contact her. She has given my name to several twins who have lost their twin and were not dealing with the event very well at all. Not one of them called to talk about it even though I knew my experience could have helped. I was disappointed and hurt for them.

About two years later I was fortunate to help my old boss with an identical situation (no pun intended). Jerry's identical twin brother was terminally ill with death expected at any moment. Throughout the ordeal family and friends gathered. On several occasions he would come over to me instead of them to talk because he and I both knew what he was experiencing. I was a friend of them both and it was obvious to me the deep level of their relationship. I hated that my brother had died but I was happy that my experience could help in a way athat no one else could offer. For that I am very grateful.

To me, facing the reality of the loss is the only way to deal with the loss. Eulogizing in my mind keeps the good memories fresh. Although that imprint in my head has never diminished, it does not come back as often. I still have those times when it still "hits" me, usually without warning. I break down and cry, mostly by myself, and then I am all right. There are times when something will occur and I will instinctively reach for the phone to call him as I so often did. I have thought of him every day since his death. I dream of him at least once a week (my dreams are another subject entirely which could take another three pages).

Nancy my wife, made a collage of photographs taken of Bill and me over the years. I proudly display it in my home. There's no need to pretend he didn't exist and that I am no longer a twin. I am still a twin!! Most people do not have a clue as to what to say or how to react when they find out I lost my twin. There's no reason to expect them to know.

I suggest the following to help other twins deal with their loss:

1. Participate in the funeral arrangements allowing the reality of death to better set in, minimizing denial. Give a eulogy if at all possible.

2. Examine your feelings and resist the temptation to stuff them by ignoring they exist. They will surface somehow anyway and this is the best way. Talk and express feelings with someone else who can identify with this special loss. Call a member of the Twinless Twins Support Group. Talking helped me the most.

3. Help someone else who has lost a close relative. You have experienced the worst loss of all and know the depths of theirs. Don't force yourself on them but make yourself available.

Sherry Nevius of Normal, Illinois, who lost her twin sister, Shawn, developed some strategies for coping which she says helped her.

A touching tribute to her twin was the drawing of a dove that Sherry had a tattoo artist ink on her skin. It was a symbol of hope and peace for Sherry, and a lasting reminder of her love for Shawn.

148

Following is Sherry's list of coping strategies:

1. Give yourself time to heal. (It took me 18 months to feel like my old self).

2. Set a goal or goals so that you have something to look forward to. I went on a trip overseas in the summer of '90. My twin sister died in August of 1988.

3. The day before my sister's wake I bought a tape---Amy Grant, The Collection. Maybe it would help others to buy themselves small gifts as pick-me-ups because every little bit helps.

4. Talk to others, especially other twins because better than anyone else, twins understand the special bond that exists among "Twinners".

5. Laughter is great medicine. It also helps to heal the hurt. A good book or movie did wonders for me.

6. Join a grief support group if you want or need others who can help you.

7. Give yourself as much time as it takes to get back to your daily living pattern.

8. You can either be your own best friend or your worst foe. Strive to get back into the mainstream of living--your twin would want it that way. But do it in time with your rhythm. Each one of of us must move in his own way.

9. Be patient with others, especially family, because unless they are or were a twin they will never truly understand the bond you had.

10. Be proud of your "twinship", once a twin always a twin. It's okay to let others know you still consider yourself a twin.

11. Keep a journal about your feelings. Writing is great therapy. Express your grief, anger, memories, and---in time---the acceptance of the loss of your twin. No one has to read your journal.

12. I worked on a painting as a tribute to Shawn and also for my own personal growth and satisfaction.

13. I had a chance to join the "Twinless Twin Group" but decided against it because I did not feel that it was healthy for me at the time to keep trying to "hang on" to my sister and wish her back to her earthly physical existence.

14. Go to church if it helps. My religious faith helped somewhat and I am grateful for it, but I did question and struggle with it more than I ever had for twelve months or so after my twin sister's death.

Can anyone, twin or non-twin prepare for the death of a loved one? I believe there are some things we can do to lighten the shock. Here are some suggestions that might be of help.

1. Recognize that the potential for loss is always present. If this thought is maintained, it should have a direct bearing on how we treat each other. Regret is always painful. It is very hard to accept, especially when it is too late to do anything about it. "If only" is an expression all of us know well. There can be less of it if we take time to express our love for others while there is life.

2. Cherish the bond of twinship. The gift you were born with is a special gift. Don't hesitate to tell your twin of your love. For some people it is hard to say "I love you" but after your loved one is gone and you can recall expressing your love for your twin, you will find great comfort. It's too late after he or she is no longer around.

3. Build a bank of happy memories you have shared with your twin. Recalling such happy times after you are alone will give you comfort in knowing the pleasure you brought one another.

4. Communicate with your twin. If you know of regrets, perhaps memories of how you mistreated your twin as a child or even in later years, be willing to say I'm sorry, if you feel in your

heart you can do so. Try to resolve old resentments and rivalries that may exist. If issues such as these have kept you from a warm loving relationship with your twin, try to let go of those feelings. The best way to have that happen is to unburden yourself with the guilt you may have for harboring such feelings. You may not be prepared for the reaction your twin will have. Be prepared for soul-searching that might come from your twin as well. Tears may flow, but they will be cleansing tears, healing tears---tears that may bring with them release and joy. Be prepared for a warm embrace (it could happen) once sharing had taken place---it could be a never to forget moment!

Twins who are left behind, parents, brothers, and sisters of twins who have died can benefit from contact with other twins and those who love them to make twin loss easier. The following sources may prove helpful to those who need some encouragement or somebody willing to listen and to share with:

National Organization of Mothers of Twins Clubs, Inc.
(NOMOTC), 12402 Princess Jeanne N. E.
Albuqerque, NM 87112-4640; (505)275-0955

Pregnancy and Infant Loss Center
1415 E. Wayzata Blvd., Suite 22
Wayzata, MN 55391; (612)473-9372

Twinless Twins Support Group
Dr. Raymond W. Brandt, Ph.D.
11220 St. Joe Rd.
Fort Wayne, IN 46815; (219)627-5414

POMBA of Canada, Inc., Parents of Multiple Births
Association of Canada, Inc.
P.O. Box 2300
Lethbridge, Alberta
Canada, T1J4K7; (403)328-9165

Tender Hearts
24134 Rimview Rd.
Moreno Valley, CA 92387; (714)924-2045

The Compassionate Friends, Inc.
P.O. Box 3696
Oak Brook, IL 60522-3696;(312)990-0010

Dr. Jane Greer, Ph.D.
Twin Consutltant
42-46 235th Street
Douglaston, NY 11363
(718) 423-9703

Twin Services, Inc.
P.O. Box 10066
Berkely, CA 94709; (415)644-0861

Minneesota Twin Loss Project
University of Minnesota
75 E. River Rd.
Minneapolis, MN 55455; (612)625-3372

The Premature and High Risk Infant Assoc., Inc.
P.O. Box A-3083 c/o West Glen Branch
Peoria, IL 61614

Multiple Births Foundation, Institute of Obstetrics and
Gynecology Trust
Queen Charlottes's and Chelsea Hospital, Goldhawk Road
London, England W6OXG;(01)748-4666, Ext.6201

TAMBA Bereavement Support Group
41 Fortuna Way, Aylesby Park
Grimsby, South Humberside, DN37 951

Jean Kollantai
P.O. Box 1064
Palmer, AK 99645, (907)745-2706

CHAPTER X

Advice To Parents And Grandpartents

This chapter is entitled Advice To Parents And Grandparents Twins. I thought it would be helpful to parents and grandparents of twins because I remember all the questions I had when my twin grandsons were born. As I was planning this chapter, I came across a document that changed my approach---because it is so delightful. It is composed of excerpts from some memories of an Oklahoma mother who raised identical twins and tells with poignant feeling the adventures of her terrible twosome. The author of this reflection is Mary Caroline Wilson who died two years ago. I have permission from her son, Jim, the remaining living twin of the pair born to Mary Caroline, to print some of his mother's remarkable insights and experiences. Her story speaks eloquently to parents and grandparents of twins who seek instruction for raising twins, and confirmation that their own trials with twins are informed passages of learning. From birth to maturity, twins are a tempestuous, funny, intriguing, exhausting and joyful adventure, as Mary Caroline tells us:

Toward the last weeks of the pregnancy, an overpowering feeling of fatigue encompassed me, and for a time my body was quiet, lulling me into a false sense of normalcy. Nature is a beguilling deceiver, for this was the last beautiful time of peace we were to have.

"Which do you want, a baby brother or a baby sister?" benign relatives and friends asked our six year old Michael.

"I really want twins, or puppies.", he invariably answered.

His reply always resulted in mirth and kidding. However, I now suspect that it either showed insight on his part or demonstrated his psychic quality, a talent which was to preserve his life many times in his future.

The smallest twin weighed three pounds and twelve ounces. This, I found, did not in any fashion represent frailty. Although, for a time I was off the track, I'll admit. Well-meaning visitors would gaze at him, particularly, and dolefully shake their heads, then launch stories about Aunt Marie's second cousin who had twins and "the smallest one died---the smallest one always dies, you know, dear. Watch him." *And watch him, we did, with all the fierceness of totally aroused parental love. But we did not reckon with the tenacity of Jim. In fact, no one, even today, upon first sight, reckons with the tenacity of Jim.*

The other twin weighed five pounds, five ounces. He seemed to be a well-adjusted, healthy baby boy, being born with one of his five senses developed way beyond the others, the sense of hunger. Even now, I accuse him of still going to the ice-box for a two o' clock feeding. To him, there was no problem which was not created by the lack of, or which could not be solved by, the consumption of a plate of food.

We plunged deep into the wells of our imaginations to come up with a name for him---after all, we had only expected a single. The gem we surfaced with, was Just Plain Bill, chosen for the most uninteresting reason that his father had always had a secret yen to have a boy called Just Plain Bill, and not because   his mother used to listen to a favorite radio serial with that title, or because she was unduly influenced by Helen Morgan, who immortalized Just `Plain Bill in song.

Both of us had a mutual horror of names which rolled off the tongues of friends in rhythmical idiocy. We made a hurried mental withdrawal from the similar sounds of Ronnie and Donnie, Berle and Earl, Floyd and Boyd, Jack and Zack, Pat and Fat, or Fred and Ted, or Sylvester and Jester. We had the noble idea that someday the twins would thank us for not denying them the right of individuality.

That was the first of a long list of mistakes on our part. They neither sought nor welcomed any claim to separate identity. On the contrary, they let us know quite early that they did not care to fraternize with other earthly creatures besides themselves, verbally or physically.

For two years we tried to establish some sort of communication with them. They seemed not to care one whit for the English language as a basis of contact between us, until one day their father decided since he provided the food and the habitat, that he was entitled to more than a grunt for a name. Thereafter, we plotted against them. We were to ignore any request unless they attempted to phrase it in English. That day of testing was a call to our separate colors.

I, the mother, suffered the most. They stolidly refused to utter so much as a vowel. I had wrested a bargain from my spouse that if they said "A-WA", he would accept that for the word "water", and we would consider that an initial victory. But they changed miraculously to camels. They went for hours without liquids. They stubbornly walked away from food, when I pleadingly offered it in exchange for a word, just any old word. (I discovered later that they squeezed water from the bathroom sponges, and the family bird dog mysteriously missed a couple of meals.)

Finally, refusing to partake of food, myself, and thoroughly exhausted with maternal anxiety, I wilted into a nap, after their own eyes were closed in sleep.

Soft whispering sounds awakened me after a time. But I did not open my eyes. I could feel movement about me and over me.

"Is she dead?" Jim asked, with perfect diction, and his voice expressed no emotion whatsoever.

"I think so," Bill said, with a faint sigh (he was always the emotional one).

"Good." Jim seemed relieved. "Let's go get in the cookie jar."

My mother love was so throttled, and my pride so crushed, that from that day forward, we had no more problems with communication. True, it could be classified as the communiques between two front lines. But they understood my hair brush perfectly.

Turbulence and chaos, inevitably, follows the birth of twins. At first, the elements of pleasure and surprise provide buoyancy. We became quite heady with the sense of accomplishment. This feeling lasted all of four hours, then the "mountain" began to grow. Expense reared its ugly head. My husband began a computation of things to come: extra diapers, extra bottles, extra, extra, extra. It

157

was overwhelming.

Feeding was my time of desperation. The physician had advised me, that if at all possible, to seek a fair method of feeding the boys since twins are in danger of missing the "mothering" which usually accompanies ordinary feeding of an infant. He suggested that I alternate their lap feedings, giving each a special little cuddly time of his own. This sounded so good, I could hardly wait to try it. But words are not actions. The house gradually became filled with sounds of my frustration, as I endeavored to fulfill "the special little cuddly time" with one twin, while the other shrieked his "cuddly " little head off. The doctor also suggested that if the first plan didn't work, I could hold them both on my lap at once, providing my lap was big enough. My lap was big enough. But somehow I could never get myself to face that. After a few weeks, the hallway which led to the twins'bedroom became known as the Corridor of Care.

Whatever possesses people to indulge in the notion that twins are no more trouble than one baby? With twins, there are two distinct babies. When you have finished bathing one baby, and fed and diapered him, and finally got him in his crib for a nap, you don't sigh with relief and sprawl into a chair for a breather. "No,no,no,no" I used to long to shout. Instead you pick up another baby and begin all over again.

And strange things can happen to this procedure, as my husband and I will testify. Interruptions can come in the middle of these routines. Memory not being infallible, and identical twin babies looking exactly alike, the same baby can get two baths, and be diapered twice while his poor little counterpart gets neglected. We have chuckled many times over this. The only thing we know we have not done for them twice is to feed them a double portion, because they can only hold just so much in their tummies.

Inevitably, the twins survived infancy and walked. When they started exploring my trials with the neighbors began.

For instance, one day a little hour of peace was shattered by the insistent ringing of my phone. A neighbor wailed into my ear,

"Mrs. Wilson, your twins won't let me out of my house to hang up my wash!"

This stopped me only momentarily, as I knew I'd be enlightened shortly. I consoled her as best I could (I've become adept at dissembling for my twins) and stepped forth to remedy the trouble.

There they sat, two steadfast little stumps on the back stoop of the house next to her's. On each side, they had a neat stack of rocks. Each time the dear, distressed lady opened her back screen door, she was pelted with rocks.

On the surface there was no explanation. Being their mother, I had definitely learned better. So I scooped them up, one under each arm, scattered their weapon-piles with my toe, and headed for the equivalent of a woodshed in our household. The tactics we employed had no resemblance to fair play. They have been established, rather, through a long series of trials and errors. The only excuse we have for using them is that they get results.

First, we put the twins in separate rooms out of earshot of one another. Then we put on our best Elliot Ness interrogation countenances (We looked grim).

For a few minutes nothing happened with the first twin. So we closed the door and went to the other twin. To him we inferred that his brother had spilled the beans, incriminating the one to whom we were talking. After a few trips back and forth, human nature being what it is, cracks appeared in their combined wall of silence. The cleavage grew. Then finally the sordid truth gushed out in one impulsive torrent.

159

This constant pitting of one against the other never caused any infraction of their loyalty to one another. To the contrary, it intensified it, and the process was a boon to us, saving us no end of wear and tear. It is the shortest line between two hard objects, so to speak.

On this occasion, when the truth emerged, they admitted that for some time they had admired the lovely rock garden the neighbor lady had in her back yard. Her husband worked for the railroad company and when he journeyed to other states he often picked up beautiful and unusual rocks for her collection. These treasures from Texas, Missouri, Illinois, Kansas, etc., had an irresistible appeal to the eyes of small boys. The barrier of a white picket fence too high for them to scale made the rocks doubly fascinating, and the obstacle created enough courage for them to go to her door and ask if they might have a few.

Of course she explained how much the rocks meant to her, where they had come from, and why she could not break up the garden, and if she gave them a few she would certainly have to give other children some also. They appeared to accept her explanation, although a trifle crestfallen.

Then they began to brood about it, and as it usually happens in such instances even with grownups, it became magnified out of proportion. So the plan evolved.

"If she won't give us any of her old rocks," they agreed defiantly, "then we will give her some!"

Not only did they sail rocks at her when she tried to come outside, they also watched for her as she passed windows in her house and attacked the glass vigorously.

When I look back, I am amazed that petitions were not signed and circulated against us in our neighborhood.

160

We did not question the turnover in neighbors in the small rent house west of us; It had a great deal to do with the twins. The father of one family who moved there in total innocence was a pistol enthusiast. He indulged in the questionable past-time of shooting rats at the city dump.

One morning his wife came to join me as I pinned the family laundry on the line. While this was not unusual, her manner was.

"Mrs. Wilson, there's something I must tell you before the children beat me to it," she began in a faltering manner. I inwardly sighed, put down my basket, and dug my heels firmly in the ground to fortify myself.

"The twins came in our house yesterday, and got Bob's pistol from the chest of drawers, and shot a hole in one of our best chairs. And while it's not at all important about the chair," she said, "we did want you to know what exactly happened in case they do tell you. We will see that the gun is not left within their reach anymore, too."

This affected me in a peculiar way. I reassured her I would redouble my already redoubled efforts to keep them out of her house, scolding them soundly for doing such a fantastic thing. We ironed out the situation, I finished hanging the clothes calmly, and went into the house and sat down. I let out a huge sigh as reaction hit me full blast. What if they had aimed the gun at one another and pulled the trigger? Nature provides a sort of built-in shock insulation in the composition of parents, but some times it wears thin.

We have never been able to count on any long stretches of peace between escapades, either. Sometimes they would come so fast on the heels of a previous one, we would still be vibrating. There was the day they locked themselves in the bathroom, and turned all faucets on full power. No amount of pleading or threatening could move them to open the door or even answer us.

161

Luckily, the bathroom had an outside window, and it occurred finally to my husband to enter that way. The lavatory had overflowed by then, and they had removed their shoes and were blissfully wading to their heart's content. When their father's face appeared at the window, and they realized they were reachable, it was heartening to hear the outlandish promises they made to thwart punishment. Needless to say we removed the locks from that particular door. This did not create a feeling of security for any guests who may have visited us, but it relieved us no end.

They moved on from their wading experience in the bathroom to their first driving test in the family auto in the same 24 hours. Thoughtlessly, my husband had left the keys in our car. We were dawdling over a second cup of coffee at the dinner table when we suddenly missed the twins. When we missed them, we never hesitated, we moved.

In this instance, we were too slow.

They had decided with three-year- old whimsy, to back the car down the drive. One moved faster than the other however, and had already turned the ignition and pressed the accelerator before the other completely got his door open. As a result, he was hanging half- in and half- out he was hanging as the car moved along. Momentarily paralyzed with fear, we watched the car gaining speed. But halfway down the drive, it swerved into the foundation of our neighbor's house with a resounding crunch. At that moment the twins vacated the car, and stood back to view their handiwork, and to giggle at the man who ran out of the house in his stocking feet to see what had happened to his home. Thank God for neighbors who appreciated the magnitude of the chore we had on our hands.

We were blessed with beauty in our neighborhood. In the circle of the twins' friends there was a small blond child named

Beth, who resembled a little French BonBon. Next door to her lived a saucy little brown-eyed Tom Boy, Jacci Lynn. Then down on the corner lived another girl with gorgeous red hair. Needless to say, boys at four and eight act pretty much the same as they do at fourteen or eighteen. Paths were worn well and wide to these homes and quite early. Weddings occurred in the neighborhood.

No wedding was ever planned with more loving care, and no father's pocket was ever spared more pecuniary picking in the process. If you loved a parade, your taste was absolutely gratified. If you had a funny bone to be tickled, you were definitely obliged. Further, if you were the sentimental type with the kind of tear ducts which are mystically stimulated at weddings, you could call upon a powerful imagination and find an infinitesimal part of that, too.

Always, following the strains of Lohengren, the first figure to come into view was the forerunner of the wedding. He was the eldest of the group, and while he found not the slightest enjoyment in his work, he obliged because he would have remained isolated and friendless for several hours if he had not. He found that more distasteful than the wedding.

He sprinted along in spurts and performed his duties in like manner. In between the spurts, he stood, brown arms akimbo, and eyed the entourage in utter disgust. During the spurts, he gave sharp hoots which put a Herald trumpet to shame. It ended up with something of the sound of "W'ding, "W'ding, "W'ding!"

Far behind him, marched the gorgeous redhead, the mother of the bride. She traveled slowly, for she liked to savor each moment of this blissful occasion with rapturous, prolonged delight. She gazed back, as often as she dared, at her incredulous handiwork. She, herself, spoiled the eye of the beholder for anyone else, even the bride. She was arrayed in a squishy purple taffeta evening dress, which boasted a V neckline that plunged almost to her eight-year-old knees. She was elevated past balance on a pair of splotched red satin French-heeled sandals. The dress was hitched up on each side to her armpits and she had chosen to conceal the large safety pins which controlled the hitches with two separated halves of a dazzling orange and brown artificial flower. Originally, it pretended to be an orchid. But its wearer decided it would possess more eloquence if she shredded its petals to resemble a giant mum. Around her white throat was a resplendent pendant of glimmering rhinestones. The pendant swayed back and forth with the movement of her body, covering most of the V neckline as it swung. As a means of anchorage its owner had hung it across the top of her ears, which made it all the more fascinating.

In her eyes was maternal pride, in her hand, a switch. This emblem was a means of reminding the bride, and all the other doubters, who was in supreme command here. Hers was the bearing of a top sergeant, a big league umpire and a four star general, all rolled in one.

Close on her heels, the little tomboy flower girl swaggered. Her bright brown eyes sparkling thorough enjoyment, she performed her duty with gusto. In each arm she bore the leaf of a huge Elephant Ear plant and she twisted forward and backward and around the bride and groom, waving the leaves as fans, and then again fluttering them slowly as part of a strange ritual dance. Obviously, hers was the purest enjoyment of the entire company. She had contributed nothing to the work. She had only stood still long enough to allow her face to be streaked with mustard in a bizarre imitation of an Indian. Her tanned, shapely legs topped with once- white shorts flashed in and out among the participants. She did not have to worry as did the mother of the bride about final effect or results. She just enjoyed it.

Correctly, according to their own peculiar code of etiquette,

164

and not Emily Post, the flower girl was followed by the ringbearer. He, as the forerunner, did not relish his position, but for the same reason (fear of exclusion) participated. Since a satin pillow could not be obtained for the ring, a dirty blue bath powderpuff had been hurriedly pressed into use. The Mother had sewn the ring on with some strong black thread.

The Mother was the ringbearer's red-headed sister and he kept his blue eyes fastened on her and the switch with the caution of a veteran, all the while marching in a sort of Goose-step fashion.

Ah, then---then the Bride and Groom. The Bride without question on anyone's part, including the groom, was ever the little French Bon Bon, looking more "Bon Bon-ish" than usual. In an ice blue satin dress (a hand-me-down from an older sister's Junior-Senior banquet and prom) and a veil of delicate lace curtain, she was a delicacy. Her eyes were down-cast. This was not due to modesty but to the fact her bare feet slipping in and out of sight under the blue satin completely fascinated her.

The twin, Bill, went unchallenged, always, as the groom. He would have faced purple dragons, including the Mother, undaunted, for this Bride. Since his feet had first trod the path across the alley, he'd loved this creature. It was the only relationship which had ever seriously threatened his closeness with his twin brother. Needless to say, she and Jim, the other twin, detested, but chose wisely, to tolerate each other.

Bill could never quite handle his emotions during the Wedding. He usually went from giggles which rose to a crescendo, to vain attempts to look very sober. All the while he clutched the Bride in a death grip. The Mother had not deemed him worthy of any special attention in the way of clothing. Typically, small interest was paid to him as the groom, his importance being only that he was the man to fill a spot at the right moment.

165

Jim, the other twin, clad in blue-jeans, tennis shoes, and a much-weathered raccoon cap, served as general all-round escort. With his bow and arrow he trotted at a respectable distance. Now and again, he left his station to scout the hills behind the garage, or the canyon behind the Spirea bushes. Anyone with a grain of Oklahoma sense knew a party of young Indian bucks might appear without warning and spirit that treasure of a Bride away. So Jim's job had importance attached. Even the Mother regarded Jim with a degree of awe.

The role of father was dispensed with. Once I weakly questioned this. The Mother replied emphatically, (letting me know by her manner that she considered the matter closed forever after), "Oh, he died or something."

"No," she had a second thought. "He was never born, I don't think." And as I said, that closed the Case of the Fatherless Bride.

He was not missed, however. The piece de resistance overshadowed all else, with the possible exception of the mother. It was a baby carriage, an English pram, holding in its depths an angelic Betsy Wetsy baby doll. It was pushed along by an anxious attending nursemaid, its presence perhaps a sign of things to come. The nurse-maid had the only fluctuating role in the Wedding. She was always recruited from the newest neighbors.

Armed with books and sage advice from our physician, we groped toward the light. The mistakes we made with our twins were mountainous. We ran the gamut of the virtues and the vices, and I might add, so did the twins. Often we were warned against making any sort of intensified comparison between the two, in weight, or in physical progress or in mental development.

We never pretended to call our talk easy, and no one would

166

believe us if we attempted to do so. We were told to try to gain some insight into the feelings of our twin children by watching them unobtrusively, in each other's company, over a period of time. This was obviously impossible from the beginning, because we could no more watch them for even a short period of fifteen minutes without getting right into the thick of it. Unobtrusively, indeed!

Then we tried to shrink our minds to their level of reasoning (for me this was no task at all) and try to find out what it means to be a twin. This had distinct advantages, and disadvantages. In some ways it was a wonderful thing. We learned:

(A) They have a playmate (I dispute that word right there before we go any further) and a companion of the same age and same interests constantly about. That must be the rub. Constantly.

(B) They are definitely the center of attraction.

(C) They have someone who shares the close closeness of all pleasures and punishments.

(D) When they are older, they can borrow and interchange clothes and toys and therefore have a much wider selection.

(E) They have the hilarious fun of fooling people if they are an identical twins.

In other respects it must be most trying to be a twin:

(A) The aforementioned bond of closeness must be smothering at times, and lead to too much dependence upon one another.

(B) The mix-ups in their identity must make them feel as if they have no individuality.

(C) The tendency for twins to become "show-offs" is much greater than for single children because too many people tend to make a fuss over them.

Our own twins went through quite a few periods of developing spurts. One would forge ahead of the other for a time in

learning. The one who lagged behind was dismayed and
bewildered, until soon he would go through the same procedure.
Raising them was an unforgettable experience. I'm glad I was their
mother.

Other twins and parents of twins have contributed items of wisdom that may prove to parents and grandparents useful in creating a philosophy for raising twins:

David A. Looney, 17, of Ontario, Oregon observed: "When all is said and done, the most important part of your children will be a reflection of what they have been taught by their parents. So be the person you would have your children be, and act accordingly; your children will follow your lead, twins or not twins."

Said James R. Hawes of Central Point, Oregon: "Show them a great deal of love, but make sure that it is as consistent and equal as humanly possible. Also, have a touching, hugging, kissing good night relationship with both parents. Do not have a permissive environment but one of reasoned limits, and responsibility should be encouraged early."

Marshall and Peggy Ann Tuttle who live in Gladstone, Oregon shared some thoughts on their experience raising identical twin girls. Peggy Ann said: "I think if I were asked what situation or aspect of raising twins was the most difficult, I would answer that I didn't really know them individually until they reached 18. Often I felt hurt that they didn't share with me. Having had a 4 1/2-year- old girl when they were born, I thought the twins and I would share the same bonding as with my older daughter. Not so! It took me years to understand that they had each other to share with. After they reached 18, they each began coming to me, one at a time, and shared their inner feelings and we began going out for dinner, movies and shopping. I will never forget when Rena asked me to go shopping and out for pizza. Honestly, I was nervous to be alone with her because we had never been together without Renee being along. We have all laughed about this aspect now but I can remember the days when I wanted to really know them and I knew I couldn't push it. Somehow I felt I had failed but I now know you must let twins set the pace. Just love them as themselves."

Hundreds of mothers, as well as some fathers, of young twins flooded me with suggestions to make life easier for parents of twins. These words of advice came from members of twin clubs that are affiliated with the National Organization of Mothers of Twins Clubs, Inc. What they say may well make the rearing of twins more enjoyable for the parents of twins who have yet to know the woes as well as the joys of dealing with two at the same time.

1. Treat your twins as individuals.

2. Get help with household chores if you can afford it (a teenage mother's helper or once-a-week maid service is a tremendous help, especially during the early months.

3. Consider diaper service instead of disposable diapers. It's cheaper ;and less time-consuming than doing cloth diapers yourself.

4. Get a sitter you can trust and-get out by yourself when you feel you need some time alone. Get out as a couple (even if it's just to take a walk).

5. Sleep whenever you get a chance (especially in the early months).

6. Watch out for the tendency to turn an older child into another parent.

7. When you start to feel sorry for yourself, think of the parents of triplets, quads, etc. Seriously, it works.

8. Speak politely to your children to receive the same.

9. A lot of prayer each day helps.

10. Take pictures of them alone when they are growing up.

11. Join a local twin club for support, encouragement, and information that relates specifically to twins. No one understands what it is like raising multiples except other parents of multiples."

From this same group of parents of twins came the following ideas and experiences that helped them to cope more successfully and happily with the rearing of their twins:

Hundreds of twins have written to me with their experiences, comments, advice to parents, and general observations. The following express some ideas and common experiences that parents of twins may find helpful.

"I find the best form of discipline for my twin children is separation, time -out we call it. When my babies were little, I found that every one in the family functioned better when I kept our twins on the same schedule, even if it meant waking the sleeper in the middle of the night. I plan to send our twins to nursery school and kindergarten, however I will ask that they be placed in different classes when they begin the first grade."

* * * * *

"My husband and I know that the presence of twins has asked us to prioritize our time. We know that for the welfare of our entire family, it is important that we have time for ourselves and for each other. We try to have at least two nights a month when we have a fun night out together. My husband feels that having twins has brought our family closer together."

* * * * *

"During our babies' first year I accepted all offers for help. After the first year things seemed to get easier as the little ones began to enjoy each other's companionship."

* * * * *

"I would recommend that every mother and father who have

170

been blessed with twins check to see if there is a support group where they live, hopefully a Mothers Of Twins club. I have found that my contact with other parents of twins has been of immense help. I thank them for the assurances which I gained from talking with others who had twins, and had Made it. They told me I could do it too. I learned that my frustration was normal; that I wasn't going crazy."

* * * * *

"The clothing exchanges were a Godsend. It was a night out for me, a social evening as well as an educational meeting. I've made wonderful friends, in fact I feel as though I am a part of one big family. My children have enjoyed knowing other twins, and the special parties have been a highlight for our family. I feel that I have been truly blessed by having twins. For me, twins are not what some people seem to think, double trouble, but rather double joy."

Having been born and reared in a totally twin environment may have prepared me for believing that that was the normal way to have children---two at a time. I never once thought of the extra work and expense, but only of the joy that was in store for our son and his wife and for my husband and me. I hesitate to make this next statement because it may sound a bit biased, but it isn't---just true. Our twin grandsons are their own individual selves who thoroughly enjoy being alone or with their twin. They are fraternal twins who do not look alike. They share many of the same activities yet have many individual interests.

I have a special message for grandparents. It comes in the form of some tips I have put together as a result of what I've learned from my own grandchildren.

1. Learn all you can about twins, and especially your own twin grandchildren. It's important for you to know if they are identical or fraternal. Why? Because if they are identical you may

have more difficulty getting to know them individually. If you understand this, you will be able to interpret their behavior more positively/ Enjoy them together, as well as separately.

2. Think of them as two people with their own unique qualities.

I will never forget the time one of my little grandsons, age 4, joined me as I sat warming by the fireplace. He settled himself up close to me and in almost a whisper ask me my interpretation of God. Those were not his words but that's what he was asking. Try to learn what each of their interests are and encourage a conversation with them appropriate to their interests. That tells them you know them on a personal level and really care about the things that interest them.

3. When you are with twins together be sure that you try to center your conversation around issues that will be of interest to both of them. Very often there is one who is more outspoken while the other is content to be entertained by the conversation going on about him. Try to draw into the conversation the child who is just listening. Let him know that what he is thinking (and he is) is important too. One of my Aunts used to enjoy telling me of a little scenerio that took place when my sister and I were about five years old---we were approached by one of her friends and ask questions. My twin spoke up and said, "This is my twin sister but she doesn't talk very much." I might add that I've made up for it over the years!"

4. When you are talking with your twins, or about them, always refer to them using their given name. When you do this you are encouraging and helping others to know them more easily and you are helping the twin children to think more of themselves as individual people rather than as a "unit of two".

One mother of identical twin girls who took part in my research told me that even though her daughters are 23 years old "their two grandmothers and grandfathers honestly have no idea of who is who. She went on to say that she was sure that is the reason the girls are not close to them now. She told me that when the grandparents see the girls they ask them "which one are you?"

5. When buying gifts for twins try to keep in mind that you are not buying gifts for the twins, but rather you are buying two gifts for two people. If you know your twin grandchildren well enough (and I hope you do) to know that they will want identical gifts, then by all means buy them the same gift. If you are uncertain as to whether they will want the same gift, don't hesitate to buy different ones for each of them that say you are your own person. Also, don't overindulge your twin grandchildren. It's fun to surprise them with a gift. They'll never know the element of surprise if you come bearing gifts every time they see you. Let the gift of 'you' be treat enough, at least part of the time.

6. Write letters, and send gifts to your twins individually. It's always fun to receive your very own letter, your very own package. Twins often are denied this joy. By doing this you are sending a subtle message to them that you see them as two individuals. But I hasten to remind you---get to know your twin grandchildren and if you observe that they like to have letters and gifts addressed to both of them instead of individually, then do what pleases them.

7. Go to 'play' with your grandchildren instead of going to 'baby-sit'. Baby-sit is not a word I use when I go to be with my twin grandsons or my three little granddaughters. Once one of them asked me, "Did you come to baby-sit?" "No, I didn't come to baby-sit, I came to play." Once a week I treat myself and spend three hours with my three little granddaughters. It's a special treat for all of us.

8. Never compare your twin grandchildren in their

presence. If you find friends or relatives comparing the children in front of them, don't hesitate to let hem know that you see each of them as unique individuals with their own talents.

9. I have saved one of the most important tips until last---and it is crucial to the happiness of the family. Make sure that the other children in the family are given equal time and recognition. Twins are often a real threat to their brothers and sisters.

CHAPTER XI

Survey Answers To Questions About Twins

What are the differences between identical and fraternal twins? Which combination of twins takes their twinship most seriously? Does it matter that we know this information? Why do men and women have different ideas about their role as twins in a family and in society? Do male and female twins have the same degree of physical coordination at the same ages? How about the timing of the maturation of social and emotional skills? Are they the same? If not, why?

These and dozens of other questions and the answers to them form the body of this concluding chapter of *We Are Twins, But Who Am I* ? The information is drawn from my survey of more than 800 twins and opens a window to some facts about twins that have not been recorded. It also may satisfy some random questions about twins that reflect the curiosity to know more about how twins feel about themselves.

Although ALL twins are interesting to non-twins, identicals have always been the most fascinating. When the word "twins" is spoken, most people think first of identicals.

And no wonder! Here are two human beings who look exactly alike, and who are often amazingly alike in other ways, too. Identical twins have been the subject of many dramas of mistaken identity, both in real life and in fiction. Often the result are comical when one twin is mistaken for the other by outsiders. But when their similarities cause confusion of personal identity within the twins themselves, it isn't always so funny. Still, identical twins come closer than any others to achieving the yet-unexplored potential for "psychic" connection between human beings.

I was a bit shocked when several of my identical twin respondents wrote that they thought fraternal twins were not really twins at all, but rather just two siblings who had the same birthday. Genetically, the last statement is true, but having the same birthday is, after all, one of the main criteria that define people as twins.

And yet, there are a few cases of twins who DON'T have the same birthday. Delbert Hass, a 50-year-old fraternal from Tigard, Oregon, wrote: "Our birthdays are a day apart, as I was born five minutes before midnight on September 29, 1933 and my brother was born 10 minutes after midnight, on September 30." I guess every rule has its exceptions!

"I would give anything to have a twin," say many singletons. Fraternal twins often say: "It would be such fun to be identical." A 29-year-old female fraternal twin from Milwaukie, Oregon recalled: "My sister and I used to wish we were identical so we could fool people. But since we are fraternal, we couldn't do anything like that."

What do identical twins say about their twinship? I almost

didn't find out. Since my research began as a personal quest, with the idea for a book occurring much later, my initial thought was: Since I am a fraternal twin, I'll ask other fraternals how they view their twinship. Only after I had designed my questionnaire did I decide that I'd also like to know about identical twins, and how they differed from fraternals.

Now I'm glad I looked into the lives of identical twins, for while they do have many experiences in common with fraternals, there are also some fascinating differences.

Because of their greater genetic similarities, the very fact that they are twins plays a much larger role in the lives of identicals than it does for fraternals. As you discovered in an earlier chapter, identical twins report more and stronger "ESP"-type connections and experiences. Even when their adult lives take different directions, the tracks of identical twins often parallel each other in remarkable ways.

Most of the aspects of twinship that all twins share are experienced with greater intensity by identicals. Because they look so much alike, identicals automatically receive more attention than fraternals, wherever they go, and the attention is more likely to be extremely positive. How many times have you heard, or even said: "Oh, look at the little twins! Aren't they adorable?"

Parents of the identicals I surveyed were more likely to call attention to their Twins' resemblance by emphasizing it with matching outfits. As children, over 95% of my identical twin respondents were dressed alike, compared with an average of 65% of fraternal twins. The figure for fraternals is somewhat misleading, however, because of the relatively low (34%) percentage of male-female twins who were dressed alike. Of same-sex fraternals, 82% were dressed alike by their parents (85% of the girls, 76% of the boys).

Both gender and twin-type differences were striking in respondents' decisions to dress alike or not as adults. Whereas 57% of identical women chose to dress alike on occasion as adults, only 33% of identical men did. Twenty-six % of adult fraternal women chose matching outfits, compared to 12% of fraternal men. Of adult male-female twins, only 5% reported occasionally dressing alike (and I suspect that those few probably limit their matching costumes to birthday parties or twins conventions).

Depending on how much they physically resemble each other, fraternal twins may receive attention for their twinship only to the extent that it is advertised---by their parents when they are young (double strollers and buggies are a sure tip-off even if the twins aren't dressed alike), and by themselves as they grow older.

The physical differences between fraternal twins can be "both a blessing and a curse." For some, it means they must find a way to make their twinship known, if such attention is important to them. For others, it means they can escape many of the pressures of comparison and the expectations of sameness, if they choose to de-emphasize their special relationship.

A fraternal female twin from Kaneohe, Hawaii, described that aspect of fraternal twinship as an advantage: "We didn't look or act alike; the thing we have in common is our voices. People were always amazed we were twins. Since we don't look alike we had the fun of being twins but not the pressure to be alike."

Proving that they are twins is much easier for some fraternal twins than for others, because fraternals vary greatly in the degree of physical resemblance they share. If they happen to have inherited many of the same genes, then they may look very much alike, making their claim to twinship more convincing. But other fraternals have very few physical traits in common, which makes their twinship harder to prove.

Occasionally, they don't even try to prove it, but instead they delight in a conspiratorial bond by denying their special relationship altogether. One female fraternal twin from Minnesota, who is now in her mid-twenties, remembered: "Because our physical appearance was so different, we used to tell people that I was adopted. Also that I was part Indian because of my darker skin tone. When traveling, my twin would tell people I was her friend that she brought along. It's fun now and then to try and convince people that we really are twins. Because we were twins with completely different physical appearances, we received a lot of attention from strangers and peers who couldn't believe we were even sisters."

While the attention that identicals receive for being twins is nearly always positive (as when people are awestruck at their resemblance), the attention received by fraternals may be much more ambiguous. The effect of this attention on their personalities and self-confidence may be quite different for fraternals than for identicals.

The more dissimilar fraternals are in physical appearance, the more insensitive are the comparative comments they are likely to hear, and the more observers may doubt their twinship. Many of these twins wrote that they often have difficulty convincing the unknowing that they are siblings, let alone twins, and not all find it as amusing as the twin quoted above.

The more fraternal twins' personalities and abilities differ, the more often they may be subjected to comparisons which discourage growth and undermine their individual self-esteem. As the personal examples elsewhere in the book illustrate, fraternal twins reported much more suffering from expectations that they be alike and comparisons of their differences. The twins themselves frequently internalized these expectations and comparisons, and doing so too often resulted in a destructive cycle of competition, jealousy, resentment, defensiveness, diminished openness and intimacy with their twin, and consequent guilt and feelings of loss. Fraternal respondents of both sexes reported more guilt about not feeling the affection and intimacy they believe they "should" have with their twin.

The genetic similarities that make identical twins look so much alike carry over to similarities in personality, interests, aptitudes, and tastes. Probably for this reason, identical twins reported fewer problems with comparisons, largely because there were fewer areas where differences could be observed and compared.

Identical twins were rarely compared on the basis of appearance, for obvious reasons. When they were compared, men were more often compared by athletic abilities, women by "personality." Both men and women reported some academic comparisons, but even these were less-threatening than for fraternals, because the differences in academic performance between identicals were usually relatively insignificant.

Though their real similarities spared them many comparisons, identicals more often reported difficulty in establishing a sense of self separate from their twin. They also reported feeling less need to do so, however, as illustrated by this comment from Robert Smith, 58, from Overland Park, Kansas: "The only identity I wanted was to be identified as Dick's twin brother, or just be the Smith Twins."

Perhaps because of the extent to which they identified with their twin, identicals were more likely than fraternals to experience intense discomfort when first separated from their twin for any length of time, with women reporting more suffering than men when their lives took different paths. Of the three categories of fraternal twins, my research shows that the female fraternal twin takes twinship most seriously. Although the emotional link between these twins is usually considerably less intense than that between identicals, their comments have led me to believe that their bond tends to be stronger and more lasting throughout life than that between male-male or male-female fraternals. Why this is, I can only speculate; perhaps it is because girls and women often seem to make more of relationships than do men and boys---whether because of biology or socialization, who knows?

If my speculation holds a grain of truth, perhaps the "feminine component" accounts for the slightly greater emphasis male-female fraternals seem to place on their twin relationship than do fraternal men. Certainly the female twins' comments in general revealed more thought given to their twinship than did the remarks of their twin brothers.

Whatever the reason, fraternal men represent the smallest group of my original survey respondents (42 individuals, out of a total of 553), compared to 75 male-female twins, 97 female fraternals, 86 identical men, and 253 identical women. Fraternal men were least likely to return the questionnaire. Their written comments were the briefest of the five categories of twins, and many appeared to feel that their twinship was a relatively unimportant influence in their lives.

Many, however, seemed simply not to have given much thought to their twinship; some were startled by their own reactions to the questions I asked. Richard M. Pittis, 24, of Edmonds, Washington, wrote: "I've been a twin for 24 years and never really thought about how it has affected me. Very interested in the results." Another man in his mid-40's wrote after completing the questionnaire: "I hope I have helped some. It's tough to sit down and write about this."

181

The fraternal men who responded to my questionnaire come from all walks of life. Among them are insurance men, teachers, truck drivers, farmers, CPAs, company presidents and other executives, ministers, pilots, students, electrical engineers, doctors, hairdressers, mail carriers, and representatives of many other occupations. Few of their co-workers were even aware that they are twins---not that they try to conceal the fact, but rather because they don't consider it an important part of their personal identity.

When I phoned one fraternal man and asked about this, he at first said: "Well, I suppose that's true. There isn't all that much to tell." Yet as we continued to discuss what it's like to be a twin, he added as an afterthought: "Well, come to think of it, there have been some feeling expressed by both of our wives about being married to a twin."

I sometimes wonder if fraternal men de-emphasize their twinship in part because such bonding goes against the traditional "masculine image" of "rugged independence." It is interesting that more than half the fraternal men I surveyed felt "in competition" with their twin as children---the highest percentage of any of the five twin-types.

Fewer fraternal men reported growing closer to their twin as they get older, and only half reported feeling closer to their twin than to their other siblings; the differences between their responses and those other types of twins to these questions were striking. Even male-female twins, who might be expected to feel closer to other siblings of their own sex, reported less competition and generally closer relationships with their twin than did fraternal men.

Male-female twins represent approximately one-third of the total twin population, yet they have not received a third of the attention given twins in the past. This is gradually changing as researchers realize the unique opportunity such twins provide for investigating the effects of gender-related treatment on children raised in an otherwise-identical environment. Because of the powerful influence of gender on status and treatment of individuals in all cultures, male-female twins have special factors to deal with in their relationship that same-sex twins do not.

Male-female twins rarely encounter situations in which people can't tell them apart. As Dorothy Caley, of Las Vegas, Nevada, said: "We didn't look anything like brother and sister, let alone twins!" These are the least likely of any twins to dress alike as children.

Male-female twins seem to have fewer problems than same-sex twins in establishing a sense of personal identity separate from their twin, probably because the gender difference is such an obvious distinguishing factor. As children they are the least likely to be given the same toys as gifts, and the most likely to be encouraged to develop separate interests. Although unwarranted stereotypes about male and female capabilities may be responsible, boy-girl twins seem to suffer less than other twins from the expectation that they should have the same interests and abilities.

Any destructive effects of comparisons between these twins usually result from the ignorance of people about the differing developmental rates of boys and girls. These differences are significant, as Nancy L. Segal pointed out in her article, "The 'Hidden' Twins" (Twins Magazine, July/August 1985): "Males tend to be heavier and longer than females, both before and after birth. Growth is faster in males than females until about 7 months of age, at which time females begin to grow faster until about age 4 years." Girls are generally quicker to develop language and fine motor skills, and they tend to excel academically in the early grades; but boys catch up and sometimes outstrip them in certain areas during the teen years.

Many of the problems male-female twins experience with

comparisons stem from the expectation that they should be equally coordinated, equally mature, or equally skilled academically, when in fact boys and girls are frequently and quite naturally "out-of-sync" in their rates of physical, psychological, and emotional development. Several of my respondents wrote of the frustration experienced by one or both twins when they were compared academically in the early grades; too often this had a far-reaching negative effect on the brother whose development of reading and writing skills lagged behind his sister.

Because of differing expectations for males and females, boy-girl twins tend to take separate paths more naturally and easily than same-sex twins as they grow older and their interests diverge. While infants, they spend as much time together as do same-sex twins. The amount of time they spend together as they grow older often depends in part on whether or not they have other same-sex siblings who are near them in age and interests. When male-female twins start formal schooling, they often tend to drift toward friendships and shared activities with members of their own sex.

Many respondents felt that their early opportunities to participate in a wide variety of play experiences, because of having a twin of the other sex, was a definite advantage of twinship. A fourteen-year-old girl from Pennsylvania, wrote: "I feel more fulfilled for being a twin, especially having a brother twin as I learn girl things and boy things."

Her twin brother noted another advantage: "She can help me with girl problems." Both men and women mentioned that their twin eased their development of friendships with individuals of the other sex.

A 33-year-old from Newport, Oregon, wrote: "We were close and able to appreciate/understand male-female peculiarities.

I've always felt it easier for me to make female friendships than male. Perhaps a twin sister eased my introduction to the other sex." This is a significant difference between male-female and other twin-types, for while the closeness of same-sex twins may make it harder for them to establish relationships with members of the other sex, the closeness shared by male-female twins seems to make it easier.

Puberty can be a confusing time for male-female twins unless they have been prepared in advance for the physical and emotional changes that will occur. One woman wrote: "I remember at the age of 13, I started menstruating and my brother tackled me and wanted to wrestle. I became very self-conscious and upset-to-tears before he realized that I really meant it. I recall his bewilderment at my not wanting to play and my inability to share with him my need to 'be a girl' and do other things."

The issues of dominance and dependency manifest themselves in special ways for male-female twins, often reflecting expectations of men's and women's roles within the society at large. As young children, the girl was sometimes favored, but this often changed with increasing age. Christine Grubb, 26, of Arvada, Colorado, wrote: "I was the dominating child. Since I was the only girl, I was able to get permission more easily for us both to do something. As we got older (18-19) I found it hard to understand why my brother was able to go more freely and with less hassle than I, just because I was a girl."

In other pairs, male supremacy reigned. "I believe I've been somewhat dominated by my twin," wrote Diane Pyle, 24, of Kansas City, Kansas. "Women's rights have not hit home in our twinship."

Both men and women spoke of the "Mother Hen Syndrome," in which the female twin "mothered" her brother in ways that diminished his ability to take responsibility for himself. This type of dependency was the most difficult aspect of separation

185

for male-female twins, as both found it hard to step out of their gender roles and relate to others of both sexes ad equals.

For identical women, dependency born of their strong emotional link made it difficult to view themselves as individuals capable of standing alone, making independent decisions, and taking actions without their twin's company and support. Perhaps this is not surprising, for of all the five categories of twins identical women were significantly less likely to report being encouraged to develop their own interests separate from those of their twin (57% said they were encouraged, compared to 76% of identical men, 78% of female fraternals, 87% of fraternal men, and 81% of male-female fraternals).

Identical twins were more likely than fraternals to choose similar careers, and to maintain close contact (professional and personal) with their twin throughout their lives. Some examples: Drs. Judy Hagedorn and Janet Kizziar, both psychologists and co-authors of *Gemini* and other books on twins; Louis G. and Donald M. Keith, President and Board Chair respectively of The Center for Study of Multiple Birth; The Rainer Twins, female duo-pianists who are profiled elsewhere in this book; and a number of "ordinary people" from my study who related parallels like the following: "My sister and I met our boyfriends around the same time. We had a double wedding. It was not planned, but our first two children, both girls, were born five days apart. Our second children were born one month and five days apart."

Among adult twins, identical men were most likely to follow parallel career paths; male-female twins were least likely to do so. Fewer women reported career parallels, possibly because among my older respondents, fewer women overall pursued careers outside the home. Of those women who did speak of their work, identicals mentioned choosing similar occupations more often than did fraternals. One woman who lives in England recalled that she and her sister "...both decided, whilst only children, that we wanted to follow teaching careers."

A comical moment was recalled by Wilma Hillegas: "One day," she said, "I was sewing and needed thread. I went to Newberry's and picked out the thread and took it over to the cashier. The clerk asked where the material was. I told her I only got a spool of thread. 'Where is the material?' she asked again. I replied, 'I only got a spool of thread.' Then she asked, 'Did you pay for the material?' 'I'm only buying a spool of thread,' I repeated. 'Then what did you do with the material?' she asked again. Just then my twin sister came to the counter with material. The poor cashier just put her head in her hands and bent down on the counter. I had not known my twin was in the store. We were wearing identical coats and hats. The same clerk had measured the material for my twin. So I finally got away by paying for just my spool of thread."

"Another time I was in the hospital and my twin sister came to see me. As my twin was leaving, the nurse got her by the arm and asked her where she was going. She said she was going home. The nurse told her she couldn't go home as the doctor wanted to do some more tests. My twin told the nurse it didn't matter as she was going home. Finally my twin led the nurse back to my room and pointed to me in bed. Then she asked the nurse if she could go home!"

While identicals can switch roles most easily, some fraternal twins resemble each other enough to pull it off. The resemblance need not always be in appearance; several fraternal female twins spoke of confusing friends and family with the similarity of their voices.

Identical twins Boyd and Blaine Cornwell of Joplin, Missouri have never married. Their lives have been so closely knit and parallel that they have consciously, and unconsciously, avoided excluding one another from most events in their lives. Careers and interests have so coincided that the two have seldom been separated.

The pair has switched roles often, and one of their favorite, harmless tricks is for one of them to order food at a restaurant while the other disappears into the restroom. Then they switch roles, confusing the waitress. They are forgiven, and the waitress is astonished, when they present themselves side by side.

Jane Thompson of Canby, Oregon, said: "My twin sister and I don't look anything alike except for maybe some family resemblances; however our voices seem to be very, very similar. When we were attending college (two different colleges), we would call home and my mother could not tell which daughter was calling. We always had to identify ourselves."

A teacher in her late thirties related with amusement how, as a teenager, she once accepted a date on her twin sister's behalf, promising all sorts of affectionate delights which caused no end of embarrassment to both twin and boyfriend until the deception was discovered. The boyfriend, now her twin's husband, still requires verification of identity, whenever his "wife's" voice makes any kind of unusual statement or request via telephone!

Identical twins can look so much alike that they sometimes even fool themselves! Helen Templeton of Lake Oswego, Oregon, told this story: "One Mother's Day, when we were about 13 years old, we had our pictures taken at a studio. Our father let us pick out the proofs, and we had individual photos mounted in a double frame. When we gave them to our mother she said, 'Oh, thank you, but they are both of the same girl!' We had to have the whole thing redone. We were embarrassed and couldn't believe we had been so dumb!"

A 21-year-old identical from Scranton, Pennsylvania, recalled with amusement: "I was shopping one day and I thought I caught sight of Sally, and I started waving. To my embarrassment, it wasn't my twin at all. I was looking into a mirror!"

It seems hard to believe that parents could fail to distinguish between their twins, yet this man in his late thirties wrote: "Our Dad died last year at the age of 89 and to his dying day he never learned to tell us apart."

An identical woman from Oregon, recalled: "Usually our parents could tell us apart without much difficulty, but one evening the doorbell rang. One of us children answered it. The man standing at the door asked for our father. When our father saw who the man was, he became so excited that he really didn't know what he was doing, and all evening he kept calling each of us by the other's name. He really had us mixed up. The man was his brother whom he hadn't seen in about 10 years!"

Even in less unsettling circumstances, family members can find their twin relatives's identities confusing. Jacquelyn Brown of Eugene, Oregon, wrote: "One day when my sister and her daughter Sarah (age 2) were visiting, Sarah got frustrated, put her hands on her hips, and cried, 'Are YOU my mommie?' Since we do live 170 miles apart, we have friends and acquaintances that don't know we are twins. We have certainly shocked many! Since we look very much alike, many are stunned!"

The man who marries an identical twin needs a strong sense of humor, for not only may he unknowingly kiss the wrong woman, he may hear rumors that his wife is stepping out on him, when in reality it is his wife's twin sister who is seen with another man.

One twin in her early fifties recalled: "My twin married first and went to Seattle to visit. I had a date, and it got back that she had stepped out on her husband. It almost cost a divorce!"

Judith Morris, 39, of Medford, Oregon, wrote: "Husbands of identical twins have to be understanding. After my husband re-decorated his office (after 12 years of marriage), I asked him why he had a wedding portrait on his desk. He replied he thought it would be nice to have my picture on his desk. I said, 'It would be, but that's not me---it's my twin!"

Identical twins often switch identities as a favor to one another. One twin who lives in Virginia wrote: "When my twin and I were in college she had mono and couldn't sign up for or go to classes at the beginning of the semester; and when she wanted to sign up late, they said no. So I went through the line twice and registered both of us. Then I went to both sets of classes and did her classwork until she was able to come back to school. Also, she was in a serious car accident a few years ago, so I went to help her family and took her kids to buy school supplies and clothes. I ran into her friends and got lots of comments about how quickly I had recovered and how they had just sent a card because they understood that I was seriously hurt!"

Another woman, in her mid-twenties, recalled: "My twin had four years of perfect attendance in high school but wanted to attend a picnic being held on a school day; so I substituted for her in class and pretended to be her. My mother called the school and said that I was ill."

"When we were in grade school, we both played basketball," wrote one 50-year-old identical man. "If one of us was in foul trouble, the coach would have us change jerseys."

A 41-year-old Oklahoma identical mentioned several instances of *trading places* : "My twin was president of 4-H. The day they took pictures she was sick, so I filled in. My first husband never knew which one of us he kissed first. During our divorce he wanted to know, but we never have told. We changed classes in high school. I liked math, she didn't. The teacher knew the difference and gave a test. My twin stood in the hall trying to get my attention for quite some time so we could change back. We had a good time!"

190

Good times like those, and the cooperation they represent, undoubtedly contribute to the close bond that identical twins often share, a bond that one 54-year-old woman described as follows: "My sister was and is one of my closest friends. It was great to always have a friend to share with and do things with."

There is no way to generalize with complete accuracy about the relative "closeness" of bonding between the individuals in the five different categories of twins. My overall subjective sense, derived from the statistical breakdown of responses to my yes/no questions and from the many personal anecdotes written by twins from all categories, is as follows:

* Identical women tend to form the closest emotional bonds and to give their twinship greatest priority throughout their lives.

* Identical men are very similar to identical women in the closeness of their bond and the importance they place on twinship.

* Of the three types of fraternal twins, female fraternals report the greatest degree of closeness with their twin and they place the highest priority on twinship.

* Male-female twins are next in hierarchy, followed by fraternal men, who often report giving lower priority to twinship than they do to their relationships with other male siblings.

It must be stressed, however, that there are many exceptions to the above patterns. Within any given category, I found twins who reported that their twin was their best friend and closest confidant. Within each category, there are also undoubtedly twins who have little to do with each other as adults.

Gender appears to be an important factor, as are other variables such as genetic similarities/differences, individual characteristics and experiences, treatment of individual twins by other people and by their twin, and the myriad other circumstances

191

that affect people's lives and development.

Each individual's life is a unique multicolored tapestry combining many threads, and it has been fascinating for me to try and discover where the color of "twinship" fits into the overall pattern.

At its best, twinship can be a give-and-take experience, a caring and sharing relationship, a "home base" from which each twin can venture out and explore the world. Twins who learn to take turns being leader and follower, who speak openly and listen empathetically, who respect each other's differences and rejoice in their similarities, can help each other build a solid foundation of individual self-esteem and at the same time cultivate in their twin "a best friend for life."

Awareness and communication are two keys to improving all human relationships, and to increase both is a major aim of this book. My research into other twins' experiences certainly has improved my own awareness and communication in my relationship with my twin. By passing on what others so generously shared with me, I hope to help other twins reap the same benefits.

Even if twins have fallen over some of the stumbling blocks described in this chapter, even if they have grown up with a less-than-ideal relationship with their twin, I firmly believe they can improve that relationship if they want to! It is my hope that this book, by illustrating the rich variety of twinship experiences, will help twins to accept themselves and their twin, and to communicate more openly than they have in the past.

It would be ideal if all twins could truly feel like the 66-year-old identical woman who wrote: "I think being a twin is the greatest blessing of my life."

But since the reality of the past in the lives of each set of
twins may have put "the ideal" beyond reach, I still wish for all my
twin readers the feeling expressed by one man in a letter to his twin
sister: "While we may not always see eye to eye, I pray we will
always see heart to heart."

Suggested Reading

Twins: Nature's Amazing Mystery, Kay Cassill. Anthenum, 1982.

The Curious World of Twins, Margaret and Vincent Gaddis. Hawthorn Books, Inc.

The Joy of Twins, Pamela Patrick Novotny. Crown, 1988.

Having Twins, Elizabeth Noble. Houghton Mifflin, 1980, revised edition 1991.

Make Room for Twins, Terry Pink Alexander. Bantam 1987.

Twins: An Uncanny Relationship, Peter Watson. Viking, 1981.

Identity and Intimacy in Twins, Barbara Schave and Janet Ciriello, Praeger, 1983.

Psychology of Twinship, Ricardo C. Ainslie, University of Nebraska Press, 1985.

The Care of Twin Children: A Common Sense Guide for Parents, by Rosemary T. Thoreaux and Josephine F. Tingley, Center for Study of Multiple Gestation, Suite 463-5, 333 Superior Street, Chicago, IL 60611.

Twins and Supertwins, Amram Scheinfeld. Baltimore, Penguin, 1973.

Twins: Twice the Trouble, Twice the Fun. Philadelphia, Lippincott, 1965..

Struggling for Wholeness, Ann Kiemel Anderson and Jan Kiemel Ream. Oliver Nelson Books, a division of Thomas Nelson,, Inc., Publishers, 1986.

Gemini: The Psychology and Phenomena of Twins, Judy W. Hagedorn and Janet W. Kizziar. Droke House/Hallux, 1983.

The Psychology of Twins, Herbert L. Collier, Ph.D. Books, Box y, 4227 North 32nd St., Phoenix, AZ 85018, 1974.

Twins on Twins, (photographs) by Kathryn McLaughlin Abbe and Frances McLaughlin Gill, Crown Publishers, New York, NY 1980.

All About Twins, Dr. Gillian Leigh. Routledge and Kegan Paul, Great Britain, 1983.

Twins from Conception to Five Years, by Averil Clegg and Ann Woolett. Van Nostrand Reinhold Co., Inc., New York, NY, 1983.

My Twin and I, Ethel M. Jones. Carlton Press, Inc., 1987.

RESOURCES

International Twins Association
1991 Co-Secretary/Treasurers
Lynn Long and Lori Stewart
6898 Channel Road NE
Minneapolis, MN 55432
(612) 571-3022

The Twins Foundation
Kay Cassill, President
P.O. Box 6043
Providence, RI 02940-6043
1(401) 274-8946
A Quarterly newsletter, The Twins Letter

The National Organization of Mothers of Twins Clubs, Inc.
(NOMOTC) P.O. Box 23188
Albuquerque, NM 87192-1188
Lois Gallmeyer, President
Quarterly newsletter, MOTC's Notebook
Current membership as of March 1991---14, 200
Number of clubs as of March 1991---400. Grandmothers,
legal guardians of multiples and godmothers are
eligible to join.

The Center For Study of Multiple Birth
333 E. Superior St., Suite 463-5
Chicago, IL 60611
Dr. Louis G. Keith and
Donald Keith, Co-directors
Features the One Stop Twin Book Shop. To place
orders write or call (312) 266-9093

International Society For Twin Studies
c/o The Mendel Institute
Piazzza Galeno, 500161
Rome, Italy
Publishers Acta Geneticae Medicae et Gemellologiae.
For more information contact
Adam P. Matheny, Jr.,
c/o The Louisville Twin Study,
Child Development Unit,
2301 S. 3rd St.
Louisville, KY 40208

Multiple Births Foundation
Queen Charlotte's and Chelsea Hospital
Goldhawk Road
London, England

Norinne Gratopp, President
Parents of Multiple Births Association of Canada (POMBA)
4981 Highway; #7 East, Unit 12A, Suite 161, Markham,
Ontario, Canada L3R 1N1
Quarterly newsletter: Double Feature

Twins Magazine
Editor: Barbara Unell
P.O. Box 12045
Overland Park, KS 66212
(913) 722-1090

Twin Services
Director: Patricia Malmstrom
P.O. Box 10066
Berkely, CA 94709
1-(415) 524-0863

Organizations Abroad

South Africa Multiple Birth Association (SAMBA)
P. O. Box 20115
Crystal Park
Benoni 1515
Transvaal
Republic of South Africa

Twins and Multiple Births Association (TAMBA)
20 Redcar Close
Lillington
Leamington Spa. Warwickshire CV32 7SU
England

Australian Multiple Birth Association (AMBA)
P. O. Box 105
Coogee 2034
New South Wales
Australia

New Zealand Multiple Birth Association
P. O. Box 1258
Wellington
New Zealand

Double Talk
P. O. Box 412
Amelia, OH 45102
Quarterly newsletter

INDEX

200